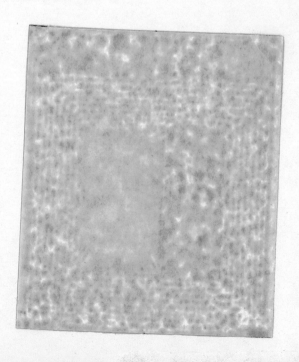

THE NATURE OF ARMS

THE NATURE OF ARMS

An exposition of the meaning and
significance of Heraldry with special
reference to its nobiliary aspects

LT. COL. ROBERT GAYRE OF GAYRE AND NIGG

K.C.N., K.C.M.M., M.A., D.Phil., D.Pol.Sc., D.Sc.
Consultore Pro Lingua Anglica, Collegio Araldico, Rome

OLIVER AND BOYD

EDINBURGH: TWEEDDALE COURT
LONDON: 39a WELBECK STREET, W.1.

FIRST PUBLISHED 1961

Printed in Great Britain by Oliver and Boyd Ltd., Edinburgh

Dedicated with permission to

HIS IMPERIAL MAJESTY OTTO OF AUSTRIA-HUNGARY

ACKNOWLEDGEMENTS

OUR THANKS are due to our good friends, of the College of Heralds of Rome, Barone A. Monti della Corte for his observations on some aspects of heraldic law in Italy, to Prof. G. Grosschmid of Visegrad, *Consultore pro lingua ungarica*, for his help on some of the intricacies of Hungarian nobiliary practices, and to Mr. Gunnar Scheffer, *Consultore pro lingua scandinavica*, and *Statsheraldiker* (State Herald) of Sweden. To Mr. Bo Tennberg are we also indebted for his observations on important aspects of Finnish heraldry as well as to the Laird of Buthlaw for observations on the drafting of patents of peerage bearing upon the use of the term " ennobling ", and to Charles Prince of Schwarzenberg for his views on certain aspects of German heraldry. Mr. F. Koller has also supplied information on demand on modern Belgian Heraldry.

We are indebted to Sir Thomas Innes of Learney, Lord Lyon King of Arms for an exchange of views over the last two years during which this book has been under consideration.

To Dr. Robert Brittain we are once again in debt for his kindness in reading the MS and correcting those innumerable errors of which an author is so frequently guilty and which he fails to observe when re-reading his manuscript.

To Mr. Vincent Powell-Smith we owe our thanks for the task of constructing the index to this book.

We wish to acknowledge the permission given by Messrs Macdonald and Company (Publishers) Limited for the reproduction of plate VIII from *Intelligible Heraldry* by Sir Christopher Lynch Robinson, and also that by Penguin Books Limited for the reproduction of plate IV from *Heraldry in England* by Dr. Anthony Wagner.

CONTENTS

CONTENTS

COLOUR PLATES

INTRODUCTION

THE SUBJECT of this book deals with what we conceive to be the fundamental basis of heraldry. If by some chance heraldry had lacked these nobiliary conceptions (which have in some realms been wholly associated with it, and, in others, very largely so) it is doubtful if it would ever have developed to become coterminous with the Christian and European civilisations. If by some chance it had, it is hardly likely to have survived with vigour over so many centuries.

Had a coat of arms been of no more value than a pretty allegorical and allusive design associated with one's name it would be of no more importance today than a rebus, merchant's mark, or trade mark. In countries where, because of their theoretically egalitarian ideas (which needless to say they do not adhere to in practice), heraldry is unrecognised, bogus arms are used with impunity. For there is no law to correct the abuse. Nevertheless, even the interest in armory which such abuses indicate is due almost entirely to the *cachet* a coat of arms is deemed to confer because of its nobiliary standing elsewhere.

In this field there has been in the last half-century a school of thought developed which has tried to divorce arms in Britain from their nobiliary anchorages. In the attempt to do this ' peasant ' arms from Switzerland, and those of mediaeval taverners and Jewish money-lenders in France of the same period, have been brought forward to prove that arms are not ensigns of nobility. Galbreath, with his background, not of Scottish heraldry, but that of bourgeois Switzerland, has been amply quoted to support this viewpoint.

All this, however, does not affect the issue, since, in the first instance, what British arms are is a matter of the law of these realms, and it would not be affected in any degree by precedents prevailing else-where. We have, we believe, set out the Law of Arms as it exists in the British realms with sufficient clarity to establish this fact. However, we believe that we have done more. For we have sought to analyse what arms are everywhere, from Central to Western and Northern Europe, and to reduce them to their various categories. The result of this analysis is to explain how and why there are ' peasant ' and ' bourgeois ' arms. We have sought to show how far they carry some degree of standing, and in what qualities they differ from noble arms in their own localities and from validly borne arms in the British Isles. The total effect of this, we hope, is to have reduced to some order, by these classifications, the standing and qualities of arms in Europe as a whole.

The final result, however, is that the nobiliary standing of arms in Scotland, England, Wales or Ireland, is in no way affected by those exceptions to our rules which may occur in other lands. Far from such exceptions destroying the status of British and other regularly employed nobiliary arms, they tend merely to prove the rule.

There has been much heat generated on this subject, and more ink spilt upon it than upon any other aspect of heraldry—most of it needlessly if the protagonists had only known their subject both in its nobiliary aspects in the British Isles and also in its wider uses throughout Europe. It is our hope that this book may do something to provide that information which will lead to a quietening of this controversy.

ROBERT GAYRE OF GAYRE AND NIGG.

Edinburgh
Christmastide, 1960

THE ORIGIN OF THE FEUDAL NOBILITY OF EUROPE AND ITS RELATION TO THE FIRST USES OF ARMS

FROM any study of symbology throughout the ages preceding the beginnings of heraldry in the twelfth century, it is evident that three primary needs were met by devices or symbols. The tribe or state and its religion made use of devices of significance to the group as a whole : leading warriors used them on their shields or clothing, their flags and their ships ; and, finally, the need for legal transactions being completed by a seal which was entirely personal, and so could bind the parties to the transaction, called for the use of personalised symbols.

The twelfth century saw none of these uses lessened in any way—but rather, on the contrary, their need was increased with the coming of the Crusades. It was probably this fact, combined with the gathering together of men from widely scattered parts of Europe, which enabled a new and improved fashion of symbology to spread rapidly throughout all parts of an international force. This caused the primitive symbology, within a century, to become the established science of armory. If there were an incipient heraldry already developing among the Moslems with whom they were in conflict, this may well have been a contributory factor.

There was, however, another important factor strongly operative at this time which had a very direct bearing on these developments— and this is an ethnological one. Europe had been overwhelmed in the preceding two thousand years by successive waves of Aryan peoples, mainly of the Nordic stock, who had conquered and settled in western and southern Europe, first as Celtic invaders, Latins and Hellenes, and later these latter had gone down before the final onslaught of

I

Gothonic and Germanic tribes. In areas where they settled thickly, as from northern Germany to England, there was no stratification of society of so marked a nature as where, in other parts, they only formed a conquering caste, as overlords, as they appear to have done in large parts of France, in Bavaria, Austria, Lombardy, Spain, and so on. But, ultimately, with the Norman conquest, England also was to partake of the same character as much of the rest of Europe, for the Norsemen, as Frenchified Normans, came in as conquerors over their distant cousins, the Anglo-Saxons. Because of this fact and the French culture which they had in part absorbed, and the right of conquest which they exercised, they formed as distinct a caste from the average Englishman of that day, as did any Langobard over the peasants and townsfolk of Lombardy.

In brief, Europe was under the heel of a conquering stock, sometimes different in race from the conquered, as in Spain and Portugal, sometimes of the same blood as in England, which formed an international fraternity in a way which we can scarcely credit today. All their pedigrees went back to the same ancestors, whether they were in the Holy Roman Empire, in France, in Italy or in the British Isles.

This led to a clear stratification of society everywhere. There was the labourer or serf, descended from the conquered. There was the townsman who was often also of the same pre-conquest period origins—but not always so in the north. Over and above these, both in their own estimation, and in fact, so far as the exercise of military and political power was concerned, were the conquerors. These were divided into the descendants of the *leaders* of the conquests of Europe and their *military following*. These two classes were freemen, and held their lands by rights of conquest, and, in the feudal system which was developing out of that very conquest itself, paid for them by *military* service. The others, the lower farmery, in the form of all manner of categories down to the serfs proper, were bound by *servile* tenure, which in its higher and more important holdings developed, for instance, in England, into some kind of copyhold or another.

Even after the passage of centuries this clear distinction between the freeman holding by military and the peasant holding by servile tenure remained, so that the gulf between the one and the other was far greater than between the aristocracy formed from the leaders of the conquests and their military followers. These latter provided such classes as those who came to be called *franklings*, and, in England, yeomen. They numbered some of those more substantial petty land-holding farmers who, in Scotland, are sometimes denominated as " bonnet lairds " because they made pretensions to lairdship although no better than farmers in real status. From the aristocracy of the conquest of Europe came the knights, the leaders in the wars, and the common run of the gentry, and those who, in Britain and elsewhere, became denominated as esquires. From the petty landowners came the men at arms, foot soldiers and bowmen. It is a mistaken concept, based upon our own ideas of armies, to think of the soldiery in general as having been from the lowest strata of society. In the mediaeval armies the contrary was the case. In the armies on the march there were, it is true, serfs with the transport to carry out the menial duties. But they did not, and would not have been allowed to take part in war. Being unfree they would have dishonoured the sword. In any case these people could claim their exemption because they served by servile and not military tenure. This difference is vividly brought out by the events of the Battle of Bannockburn in 1314. The army led by the Scottish king consisting of horse and foot, ranging from the aristocracy down to the freemen, faced the English army, while in the rear, at a considerable distance away, remained the camp followers or servants. It was they, in order to see how the battle was faring, who assembled on a nearby hill. Imitating their betters they did so in a mock military formation. This caused the dispirited English force to lose all the morale it had left, for it thought another army was advancing upon them.[1]

This distinction between the noble free service of the army and servile status persisted long after feudalism passed away. We find, for instance, Richard Jhones, in *The Booke of Honor and Armes*, printed in London, 1590 (Third Book, p. 36), saying—" A soldier that hath

---

[1] Since writing the above we find that General Sir Philip Christison has stated that these people were not serfs and menials, but irregular troops. If so this strengthens our point as to the free character of most of the personnel associated with mediaeval armies. *Bannockburn; The Story of the Battle*, National Trust for Scotland, Edinburgh, 1960.

B

long served without reproach ought to be accompted a Gentleman"
(that is a noble). This high estimation of military service survived
particularly in the cavalry, so that every private trooper could consider himself a gentleman right down to the mid seventeenth century
and later. As a consequence Dick Steele did not lose caste by serving
as a trooper. The concept of the high and genteel calling of the army
persisted even longer with the Highland regiments. In these not
only had every private soldier the sword (claymore), but in the baggage
trains there were servants for the soldiers as well as their officers.[1]

In such a feudal organisation of society as we have been discussing
the people who held their lands and rights by servile obligations had
to give service on the demense lands and, perhaps, by making certain
payments in kind. They also had to be subject to the jurisdiction of the
manorial courts to which they belonged. While those holding lands by
free service had the right in most principalities of direct appeal to the
overlord's jurisdiction. This became somewhat complicated later, when
freemen acquired copyhold or similar lands and held these by non-
military service, apart from those lands which they held by freehold
obligations. But, broadly speaking, at the beginning and for a long
time thereafter there tended to be a segregation of these two types of
landowners, although, often enough, a free landholder might be little
better in his economic status as a farmer than many of the richer
copyhold and non-free tenants.

It should also be observed that for a very long time it was not
possible for a man, no matter how rich he might be, to acquire land
held by military tenure, if he himself were not noble, or at least a
freeman, already holding lands by that service.

Manors and feudal baronies were normally held of the Sovereign,
but they could also be held in certain realms, if not in all, of one of
his great magnates, lay or ecclesiastical. In such cases where the
vassal held the whole of the manor or barony, he was a baron, but

[1] In Scotland the feudal service tended to be somewhat different from that which we
have described, as it grew in a freer society, and there were no Norman conquerors and
unfree " natives ". Consequently in that country the vassals of an overlord (excepting
perhaps for cotters, labourers and small farmers) all had military services to perform. An
important exposition of the Scottish form of feudal service will be found in—Wm. Croft
Dickinson's *The Court Book of the Barony of Carnwath, Scottish History Society*, 1937.

holding of the magnate and not the prince. In this way, for instance, the Church in many places built up a considerable military force of its own. Sometimes, however, the magnate, lay or ecclesiastical, retained the *caput*, usually the hall of the manor, for himself, and in that case the tenant was not the lord of the manor, although he was tantamount to baron in extent of lands and power. Sometimes a barony would be split between portioners, such as when daughters inherited portions equally of the fief.

In addition, a barony or manor might be deliberately split into one or more portions, and feued out by the superior to vassals. This was subinfeudation, and when it occurred the holders were holding *in vavasoria* of their immediate feudal superior who owned the whole feu, and not of the Crown or other overlord direct.

While all land held by military service was free or noble land, in some realms an inhibition was placed in general practice on how far it was considered a noble fief, when so split up, and so as to how far it could convey to its holder nobility of rank. Consequently, it was often held that where subdivision went beyond subinfeudation, it ceased to confer noble status *per se*. In England, actually, steps were taken to prevent subinfeudation altogether, although this was not the case in Scotland—but even here it was probably limited to *in vavasoria*, so far as conferring noble status was concerned, since it would be unlikely that any smaller holding would have been sufficient to maintain the " horse and harness " which was required in the service of the Crown from a noble. It should be remembered, in regard to the last point, that while it was only the man in armour, an esquire, who was counted by name in the enrolment, being a gentleman, he would often have with him his own small following of free or military companions—probably a couple of men at arms, or bill men or archers raised from poorer kin, or from yeomen, and several menials as well.

In passing, it might be observed, that a manor or barony might not only be held by someone without the caput, or held in portionership, or sub-divided in portions as *in vavasoria*, but on other occasions, a part of it might be detached completely as *free tenandry*, leaving the rest still the manor proper. This did not reduce the two parts, the free tenandry and the barony which was left, to holdings *in vavasoria*.

For the free tenandry now came to have an independent existence. The charter establishing it had to have the prince's consent, and it usually freed the tenant of obligations to his former overlord or put the tenancy on some new footing. Meanwhile the land comprising the rest of the barony in its turn could be subdivided *in vavasoria*.

It will thus be realised that the lands which conferred noble status need not, in the end, be as vast as the original feudal barony—at the beginning usually a very considerable estate—but would, in many cases, be like many country properties and smaller estates of today. The result of this was that the class which was noble was a numerous class, and by no means restricted in numbers to the few who today are peers of the realm. They were, in other words, just as numerous as that class nowadays which considers itself to be the *gentry*.

While in certain realms, such as England, where subinfeudation was prohibited, and in Scotland where it was below the rank of vavasour, it is doubtful how far such land-holding could confer noble status,[1] in other realms subinfeudation still retained for its lands nobility of status. This seems to have been the case, for instance, in Sicily.

In practice, we suspect that it would not matter whether the land was held *in vavasoria*, or even *in subvavasoria*, or even a lower subinfeudation, as long as it was extensive enough to supply the man-at-arms with his horse and harness, and such small following as went with that supply. The statement that all who acquired land in Scotland, and could furnish man, horse and harness, could be considered noble and acquire also a coat of arms, seems to suggest that this was the practical criterion on which nobility rested.

The result of all this is that that we have the concept of a *caste* which had overflowed every western and southern European country. In the course of doing so it had established feudalism. Under this system it was a free class, held free lands, and provided the military defence of the realm in all ranks from that of the great magnates (later to be known as bannerets[2]) down to simple gentlemen and esquires.

---

[1] Although every parcel of free land, since it was part of a noble feu was held by military service, and conferred frankling status at least.

[2] See Gayre of Gayre & Nigg, *Heraldic Standards and other Ensigns*, Oliver & Boyd, Edinburgh, where the whole question of banners, and the position of bannerets, is discussed.

Below the strictly noble class of chief tenants and vavasours were the military followers of the noble. These were sometimes mounted as men-at-arms, but more often than not they were billmen and archers. These freemen came to be known as the yeomanry. They were, at first, racially the same as their superiors, and they held their lands by obligations which were of the same nature and kind as those by which their superiors held. The distinction, therefore, was not a very great one. We can see how relatively artificial was the distinction when we remember that in England younger sons of noble houses, who had a right to their own coats of arms, and to be received as kin by the chiefs of their houses, would, for all that, residing on their small freeholdings, describe themselves as *yeomen* on some occasions and on others as *gentlemen*.

It is quite clear that the distinction which existed in some countries (such as England and Scotland) between the tenants in chief and their vavasours, and the rest of the franklings, or freemen, holding by military tenure, was much less apparent at certain periods in other lands. We believe that in countries which have a strong *bauer* or *yeomen* tradition, where the free farmery generally entrenched themselves early, and had rights of being heard, and later of representation, in local, and ultimately national councils, there was a very strong tendency not to draw so marked a line between the noble and the non-noble freeman. In such lands the latter were in some sense nobles—although of a very petty noblesse. Elsewhere they would certainly not have been so received. We believe that this was the situation in parts of Switzerland, the Low Countries, and north-eastern France.

Among the nobles the concept of knighthood arose, and so it is not surprising to find that in England the manors are rated by their value in terms of knight-service—that is how many knights, or proportions of a knight, and their following needed to perform their duties, were to be provided for the fiefs involved. Elsewhere, such as in parts of Germany, we also come across much the same system.

These, therefore, are the socio-ethnological foundations of mediaeval European society, found in some degree or another everywhere outside of Eastern Europe. There, in certain countries, other conditions tended to prevail. Although even there they were being strongly influenced all the time by these conditions of which we speak.

It will be observed that feudalism and knighthood existed before the origin of coats of arms, in a defined and scientific system such as we now have it in heraldry. For this was already the pattern of Europe which was taking shape by the time of the Norman Conquest and in the following century.

When, however, arms began to be used in the sense which we can consider heraldic—that is when a man bore a device on his shield

Count of Flanders   Dr Anthony Wagner   Geoffrey Plantagenet
                                                  Count of Anjou

consistently throughout his life, and then transmitted it to his heir—it is obvious that they must have been adopted by the leading magnates of the day, and not by the lower echelons of the feudal nobility. For it is only a man in a superior position who would venture to introduce new ideas, and blazon them forth in the army, in civil life and at court. Anyone of lesser rank would have risked a reproof. This is confirmed by what we find. For the earliest sporadic evidences of the first heraldry are all associated with great names. Thus, Cussans[1] draws our attention to the fact that one of the earliest well authenticated evidences of heraldry is found on a seal of 1164 of Philip, Count of Flanders (a sovereign prince) who has the lion rampant which

---

[1] John E. Cussans, *Handbook of Heraldry*. Chatto & Windus, London, 1882, p. 21.

we know continued thereafter. Dr. Wagner,[1] too, points to an even earlier use of arms in connection with Geoffrey Plantagenet, Count of Anjou, who received a shield from Henry I of England in 1127 on which were charged golden lions, which may be the forerunners of the 3 leopards or lions of England. We have, however, to come to the Third Crusade, 1189, before we find a general spread of the use of heraldry in the European armies. Even in these cases we are in the main dealing with leading personalities from each European country and province rather than the rank and file of the nobility, and it is probable that it was another century, the thirteenth, before arms had become general to all nobles in Western Europe, and it was not till the fifteenth to all Hungarian nobles.

From what we have said it is clear that while nobility preceded heraldry, the possession of arms was located, at first, in the higher nobility and only eventually penetrated downwards to comprehend the whole of the noblesse.

[1] Anthony Wagner, Richmond Herald. *Heraldry in England*, The King Penguin Books, 1946, p. 6.

THE PRESCRIPTIVE RIGHT TO ARMS

AT the period with which we have been dealing —the twelfth to the thirteenth centuries, when arms were becoming general—it is quite clear that arms arose *prescriptively*. They were adopted at the pleasure of their users, discarded when they did not suit, and others assumed, until in process of time the idea had become established that arms could no longer be treated in that way and had to be accepted as hereditary. But, all along in this period, arms were adopted at the instance of their bearers.

Since, as we have shown, arms arose among great magnates they became associated with the nobility, and their bearing was related to that rank. As a result, coats of arms began to be considered as the symbols or evidence of nobility, and thus they came to be so called, as *tesserae nobilitatis* or *tesserae gentilitatis*, signs of nobility or gentry. Once that relation to rank was established it was a presumption for anyone other than a noble in the feudal army to use them. Once this association between arms and nobility occurred there obviously arose the need to control their use. That meant some person or government machinery was needed. At first, there is little doubt, such control was exercised by the overlord himself in person, the Earl, who was a Prince in his own Earldom, would settle disputes and make regulations among his vassals, lords, barons, knights and gentry. Indeed, not only did the superior govern in some measure the bearings of his vassals, but he sometimes gave to them a part of his own arms, as an honourable augmentation to their existing arms. A well-known example of this, to which we have referred in *Heraldic Cadency*, is the case where Lord Audley gave from his own coat of arms of *Gules a fret Or*, to his two esquires Mackworth and de Delves, *a chevron Gules frety Or*. As the

conception that arms were the veritable and outward signs of nobility
became established it followed that they had to be conferred on those
who rose from lower origins to confirm them into the ranks of the
nobility.   For, although we have spoken of the socio-ethnological

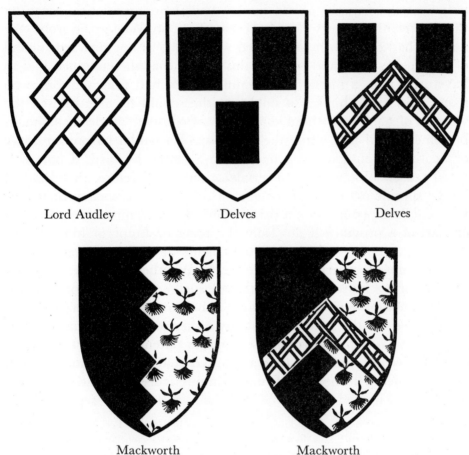

Lord Audley   Delves   Delves

Mackworth   Mackworth

caste system of the Middle Ages, it is obvious that there would, and
did, arise from time to time, situations in which a person of ignoble
origins, for some merit of his own, or some opportunism which he
practised, succeeded in enfranchising himself, and from that stage
progressed until he was actually ennobled.   In some countries, such
as Germany, Hungary, France and Spain, we have extant many of
the actual patents of nobility which were granted.   These were

particularly the reward of rich burgesses of the cities, for the towns
were progressively becoming more powerful. Consequently they were
able to exert their influence by the usual means by which capitalist
pressure succeeds, in so many cases, in taking over the control of the
nation at the expense of the landed feudal organisations. Since by
the thirteenth century almost everywhere in Western Europe the
nobility had come to be associated with arms, as the outward symbol
of their caste-rank, and because this meant that the ennobled had to
have arms also, a method of obtaining them had to arise. Since no
man could make himself a noble, neither could he give himself the
symbols of nobility without some form of consent. Indeed, it should
be remembered that while the purchase of a feudal barony in Sicily
or Scotland would make a man already noble by birth a baron, it
could not ennoble anyone of servile origin.[1] Therefore, there had to
be the specific act of ennoblement. Constructed as society then was,
this could only come from a prince, perhaps the semi-sovereign Count
or Earl of a province if not from the King or Emperor himself. In
some cases, having achieved ennoblement, the right of prescriptively
creating one's own arms was allowed.[2] Whether this was a general
practice or not for such provinces where such a thing could be possible,
does not matter very much, because it became normal everywhere as
time passed for the patent of nobility either to confer a coat of arms
within the same patent, or for a separate patent of arms to be sued
out. It became the view that a granted coat was superior to a self
assumed one.[3] In the Holy Roman Empire it seems that the granting
of the arms tended to become detached, and treated separately, as

[1] Scots Law required every landowner to have a coat of arms, 21 Feb. 1400, Acts i, 575 ;
1430, cap. 21, Acts ii, 19. This does not, however, mean that a plebeian could acquire land
which required military service (and so the use of arms).

[2] Nicholas Upton, as follows in the *Book of St. Albans* says . . . " many poore men by thayr
grace favoure laboure or deservying ; ar made nobuls . . . and of theys men mony be theyr
awne autorite have taken armys to be borne to theym and to ther hayres . . ."

[3] W. H. St. John Hope. *Grammar of English Heraldry.* Cambridge, 1913. P. 85, concludes
that it is clear that by the time at which Upton was writing (fifteenth century) the prescriptive
assumption of arms by the newly created noble was not considered as desirable as a concession
from the King (which meant that the arms were protected with all the force of law) for Upton
says :—" Bot yit they be not of so grete dignyte and autorite as those armys the wich ar
grauntyt day by day by the autorite of a prynce or of a lorde ".

we shall see later, from that of nobility, although both might be contained in the same deed. In contrast, however, in Scotland, England and Ireland, there is no doubt, as we shall show later, that the two acts were in the one patent, once the period had entirely passed for the prescriptive assumptions of arms. This became known generally in the British Isles as a grant of arms. It should be observed that this also became the custom in Italy, where, since the late sixteenth century the Italian sovereigns began to issue grants of arms in their letters patent of nobility.[1] While in Sweden, as we shall point out later, as well as in other states, the same thing is true.

The outcome of this was that since the ennobled had to have recourse to the sovereign for nobility and arms it followed that, whatever claims the established hereditary nobility may have made for the antiquity of their names, styles and arms, and their prescriptive rights in these latter, they too would inevitably be forced to conform to royal or princely control. For, if an ennobled man had to have a patent of arms, it would in time become established that a noble could not change his arms at will. Naturally this took time before it became the custom and then the law.

Another factor also began to be operative arising out of the superior's control of his vassals' arms. The two uses of arms were in war and in law : on shield and ensign, or on seal. This led to the creation of officers of arms to record before a battle, or at the commencement of a campaign, all the *arms* (that is nobles who were thus designated by their arms) enrolled under each commander. This fact of enrolling the arms, on those magnificent rolls of arms many of which have survived, by its very act brought arms under the jurisdiction of the Prince, and feudalised them. Where there might be conflict in the coats borne, or not sufficient differences observed, or any disputes which were likely to arise between the armigers and his heraldic officers appointed for the task, the court martial under his presidency would be called upon to adjudicate.

[1] It should be observed, however, that in the concession of fiefs no mention of arms occurs, nor in those of titles of feudal lords (which went with the lands). This is because no one could possess a fief who was not already noble, and possessed arms. Consequently, the concession of a fief and title only involved, *armorially*, the addition to his existing arms of the coronet of his new rank.

Plates II and IV are examples of arms from such a roll. In this case they are from the fourteenth century *Armorial de Gelre*, which is of some importance in Scotland for the Scottish arms which it displays. This roll was composed by the herald of the Duke of Gueldres, Claes Heynen, between 1334 and 1372, to which additions have been made later. It is deposited in The Royal Library in Brussels.

However, to return to the matter in hand, it is evident that the forces which made up the life of the Middle Ages had, by the thirteenth century to the early fourteenth century, contributed towards establishing a royal feudal supremacy over arms. In Scotland there is a record of a Lord Lyon King of Arms being knighted at his inauguration in 1318 by Robert I (the Bruce). From this date we can consider that any ideas of prescriptive right would be subject to the scrutiny, if not the actual control, of the King of Arms. Although it would, undoubtedly, be much later before prescription became a dead letter. In England we have a mention of a King of Arms for North of Trent (Norroy) by the time of Edward I (1272-1307), and in Ireland a King of Arms by 1382, and we can assume that these dates must represent the period at which prescriptive rights were under challenge if not absolute control. By the time we come to the reign of Charles VI in France, we find, in 1406, the erection of the heralds into a chartered corporation, and by that of Richard III in England, in 1484, the foundation of the College of Arms by a similar incorporation. It is at this point that we can infer that the opportunities for any building up, *de novo*, of claims of prescriptive rights to arms must have been definitely drawing to an end.

What remained, no doubt, was a right, on long user, to arms which had themselves arisen prescriptively, even if these prescriptive arms had not been recorded in any royal rolls of arms either on the battle-field or in the incorporated bodies or courts of heraldry. It is quite clear that the Crown never disputed that there were such arms. The writ of Henry V, in 1418, to the sheriffs of the shires of England, makes it clear that while on previous expeditions he had found that some had assumed to themselves arms in cases where they and their forebears had not previously used them, no one should assume such arms, *unless he had them from his ancestors*, or ought to possess them by right of ancestry, or by a patent or gift from a person empowered to bestow arms, or had borne arms at Agincourt[1]—which arms were to be accepted as legitimate. Mr. L. G. Pine[2] is quite right to stress that this writ does not debar arms which had arisen by prescription. Obviously it could not do that since most ancient arms of the original nobility of Europe had arisen in this prescriptive manner. But what it did do was to put a prohibition upon further prescriptive rights being created at that time, 1418, and we think it would be putting too fine an edge on the matter to suggest that the writ means that it only referred to that one occasion. It seems evident that from this time onwards we must reconcile ourselves to the view that the Crown was determined to control the use and creation of arms in England.

The *Boke of St. Albans* is often quoted as evidence that any man might take arms. But this is a misquotation as it specifically states any *Nobulman* may.

Thus Upton (or whoever he was)[3] in the *Boke of St. Albans*, says— " as in these days we see how many poor men . . . have become noble . . . and many of these have taken arms to be borne by themselves and their heirs ".[4] From this it is quite clear that the achievement of a noble status was involved with the assumption of the arms by the fifteenth century when these words were written. (Upton died before 15.7.1487.)[5]

Therefore, it is a logical development from what we have seen above, to find in the sixteenth and seventeenth centuries the institution of visitations in England. These sent the heralds to every bailliwick of the realm to record the arms of those who could prove their right to them from their ancestors (which would be in most cases by ancient

---

[1] Barron, Fox-Davies, and most other writers have assumed that the arms used at Agincourt were assumed prescriptively at that time. Mr. G. D. Squibb, *The Law of Arms in England*, Heraldry Society, East Knoyle, Wilts., 1953, p. 7, contests this view, and argues that the exception was made in favour of the armigerous men of Agincourt because, on that occasion, they had made good their right to arms.

[2] *Heraldry and Genealogy*. The English Universities Press Ltd., London 1957, p. 65.

[3] Evan John Jones. *Mediaeval Heraldry*, Cardiff 1943, gives a good account of the authorship of the mediaeval work associated with Upton's name.

[4] This is the same passage as we have quoted in the original in note 2.

[5] *Ut supra.*, p. XXIV.

user of prescriptive arms), and stop those who had in recent years
or on very recent user come to use prescriptively self-assumed arms.

The Act of 1592 of the Scottish Parliament is obviously an attempt
to do exactly the same thing, and it sets out—" Our Sovereign Lord
and Estates of this present parliament, considering the great abuse
that has been among the lieges of this realm in their bearing of arms,
usurping to themselves such arms as belong not unto them, so that it
cannot be distinguished by their arms who are gentlemen of blood
of their ancestors, nor yet may be seen what gentlemen are descended
of noble stock and lineage, for remedy whereof His Highness, with
advice of the said Estates, has given and granted, by this present
act gives and grants full power and commission to Lyon King of
Arms, and his brethren heralds, to visit the whole arms of noblemen,[1]
barons and gentlemen borne and used within this realm " etc.   In
point of fact this act failed in its objectives and it was not until the new
act of the Scottish Parliament of 1672 that the Sovereign finally established his full and absolute control over heraldry in Scotland, with
power to the Lord Lyon to fine in One Hundred Pounds all who un-
justly usurped arms.[2]   Since this time all arms in Scotland are
feudalised, however they arose before that period, and are feudal
heritage as much as a barony or a castle.   They are incorporeal fiefs,
and so incorporeal heritage,[3] while a grant of arms, as it was in old
France, is a *fief annoblissant*, whose possession ennobles.[4]   To which
latter subject we shall return later at some length.

In England the visitations started in 1530, under Henry VIII, and
continued till 1688 under James VII and II.   In Ireland, probably

[1] The old Scottish and English use of the term *nobleman* was for any noble, whether *peer*,
baron (or *lord of manor*) or *gentleman*. By Tudor times in England a restricted use to *peers* was
beginning to become common, and by late Tudor times was beginning to be used in Scotland.
It seems to be used in that sense here. However, Scottish heraldic practice has returned
to the older historic, and international, use of the term, using nobility for *noblesse*, of which
the peers are only a part.

[2] For the text of both these acts see—Sir Thomas Innes of Learney, *Scots Heraldry*, Oliver
& Boyd, Edinburgh. 2nd. edition, pp. 239 ff.

[3] J. Woodward, *Heraldry, British and Foreign*, pp. 8, 11 and 15.

[4] " . . . it is necessary to point out that in most ancient realms the concept of nobility has
been related to the tenure of *noble terre* and that arms are regarded as incorporeal *fiefs annoblissants*." Innes of Learney, *Scots Heraldry*, Edinburgh, 1956, p. 22.

owing to the difficulties of carrying them out, there were only three visitations, which took place between 1606 and 1618. It will, however, be observed that in all three countries it is in the sixteenth and seventeenth centuries that the efforts for control were made by the Crown. In Piedmont we find similar visitations instituted in the seventeenth century.

Resulting from this we have been left with two quite distinct practices. The first is that which is found in England. If we have rightly understood the theory of modern English practice it is that no arms, not found in the visitation records, or other legal proofs of existence in the College of Arms, can be accepted as genuine and allowed. That this will be so in a vast majority of cases there is no doubt. But, it does not allow for the possibility, of which instances no doubt could be cited, in which a family for one reason or another was not enrolled at the visitations, but which had used arms for generations, whether by prescriptive right, or a grant the record of which had been lost. Extinction of a male line, transmission of its estates to heiresses, and the down at heel condition of cadets, who had sunk into the yeomanry, could all account for a failure of arms to be recorded at that time. The second is that which is common to the Irish and Scottish practices. These have allowed for that eventuality, as they have continued to exercise the right of confirmation of arms, the rights to which can be shown to be based, in the former case, on the user of three generations or more, and in the latter where it can be shown that the arms have long user and were probably already in use from very early times contemporaneous with the Acts to which we have referred.

The Court of Chivalry of Scotland has continued to function unimpaired since the Middle Ages, and has been fortified by a series of Acts of Parliament of the sixteenth, seventeenth and nineteenth centuries. Consequently, it has not been possible for anyone to argue that a prescriptive right to arms can be created subsequent to that long evolutionary period from the time arms were first created until the authority of Lyon Court was finally and firmly established by the first of these Acts of Parliament, and subsequently strengthened by the succeeding ones. In contrast, in England, there has been a school which has argued that, with the ending of the visitations, followed by the failure of the Earl Marshal's Court to sit after 1735, and the absence of machinery in that realm whereby the Laws of Arms could be enforced, *ipso facto*, prescription had come back into existence. Whatever substance there may have been in this argument was destroyed by the action brought by *The Lord Mayor, Aldermen and Citizens of Manchester* against the *Manchester Palace of Varieties Ltd.* before that Court in December 1954, when it sat for the first time since 1735, tried the case and delivered judgment. Therefore, as there is the machinery of the court, and as it has been used, and can con-

City of Manchester

ceivably be again, there exists the institution which can redress wrongs where they have been committed in matters armorial. Consequently, in the realm of England just as in that of Scotland there is no argument which can be based on a continuing right to establish a prescription *de novo*. The only one which can possibly be put forward is where there was a very ancient prescriptive right, and continued long user since, which for certain reasons (which would have to be shown most cogently before the court) had not come under the legal cognizance of the King of Arms.

As a matter of convenience Ulster laid it down that he was prepared to accept 3 generations (and this has sometimes been interpreted as sixty years) to establish user. It can, therefore, be argued, and is, that a man may create his own arms, and his grandchildren have them legalised. No doubt this is sometimes done, but we do not believe that is what was really intended by the Irish heralds when this formula was first adopted. The user of 3 generations was, we have no doubt, a useful and reasonable yardstick to cover a period which would come within the knowledge of the petitioner. A similar principle was operative with the English heralds, since Sir William Dugdale issued an instruction between 1683 and 1686, giving the period as eighty years for establishment by user. We are quite certain in our own mind that the intention was to take the arms back to a sufficiently early period when it was known that all arms had not been recorded—that is around the end of the sixteenth and the beginning of the seventeenth centuries.   If it could be proved that a family had used arms in the 1680's which had been in continuous use from the end of the sixteenth century they were given the grace of the College of Arms, and allowed those arms, on the assumption that public opinion would not have tolerated uninterruptedly this use for this period of time if it had been flagrantly improper. We doubt, therefore, whether it is not defeating the intention of the " three generations " not to expand these by every generation since about 1680. Consequently, although the Irish heralds may have very generously allowed the three generations to count back from any date subsequent to the 1680's, this would appear to be only an extremely generous act of grace, and not something on which to base a continued right even in Ireland for continuous and ever newly created prescriptive rights.

It has been argued that there is a prescriptive right to arms in states where there is no legislation for the control of arms, and developments in recent years have taken place in both Germany and America [1] in this direction. Concerning this we shall have something to say later when we come to discuss the surviving nature of arms in certain states today.

[1] We venture the opinion, for what it is worth, that all bishops, deans, chancellors, and other high officials of the Protestant Episcopal Church of America are entitled to petition H.M. Lyon Court for arms, on the ground that that Church is a daughter Church of the Episcopal Church of Scotland from which it derives its succession. In that sense they can claim to be dignitaries within the ambient of the Scottish mother Church. In the same way it seems to us, any bishop of the Church of India, Ceylon, Burma and Pakistan, as an off-shoot of the English Church should be able to petition the College of Arms, despite the fact that he might not be of English blood or nationality.

C

CHAPTER III

THE NOBILIARY STATUS OF ARMS IN SCOTLAND IN THE 16th, 17th AND 18th CENTURIES

WE have seen, thus far, that in the Middle Ages we have been dealing with a ruling caste which held fiefs from overlords, and ultimately from the Prince of each realm. These nobles were *alt-* and *ur-adel*, holding their nobility from the earliest times. We have seen that at a later stage the ennoblement of simpler folk took place, and although in the earlier times some did assume their own arms, these generally were granted, whereas the original nobility had in the beginning generally assumed their legally recognised arms prescriptively. This was not, however, invariable. It seems that there were instances in which noble families (or branches of such families) either did not bear arms, or bore such arms as were not admissable by the Crown once it had assumed the full control of heraldry. For it seems clear from the Scottish Act of Parliament of 1592 that Lyon was restricted to granting arms to nobles only—from which it would seem that there were nobles who were still in need of admissable arms. This fact led that great Scottish heraldic authority and Lord Advocate, Sir George Mackenzie of Rosehaugh,[1] when commenting on this Scottish Act of Parliament of 1592, to say that " it is observable that Lyon cannot give Arms to such as are not Noble by descent ; for the reason inductive of this Statute is, That there may be a difference betwixt such as are Noble, and such as are not ; but there would be none, if it were lawful to the Lyon to give Arms even to such as are not Gentlemen by birth : For as he cannot Nobilitate, so neither can he bestow the marks of Nobility. Likeas, by that Act, he is commanded to inhibit all such as are not Noble to carry Arms ".

[1] Sir George Mackenzie of Rosehaugh, knight. *The Science of Heraldry*, Edinburgh, 1680, p. 12.

It is important to observe that while Lyon could under the Act of 1592 give arms only to Nobles, the Act is equally specific that arms could only be borne by nobles, for it states that the duty of the heralds is " to put inhibition to all the common sort of people not worthy by the law of arms to bear any signs armorials ".

In further support of his last point Sir George Mackenzie of Rosehaugh also says elsewhere, " From which Act, we may draw these Conclusions, That only such as are Gentlemen by Blood can carry Arms ; which opinion is also received now into the Laws of Nations, Hopp. cap 6. Par. 10."[1]

From these clear statements it is quite evident that so far as Scotland is concerned, both explicitly stated in the Act of 1592, and the comments thereon of the Lord Advocate, arms are *insignia of nobility and non-nobles cannot carry arms.*

Mackenzie of Rosehaugh

From which it follows that in Scottish law those that do are nobles.

It should, however, be realised that this statement of heraldic law in Scotland, as given by Rosehaugh, refers to the position of affairs in Scotland as it was under the Act of 1592, and before the Act of 1672.[2] Mackenzie of Rosehaugh was largely responsible for bringing on to the Statute Book this latter Act. It materially strengthened the position of the Lyon Court, brought it up to date, and enabled it to control new precedents which in the meantime had come to be accepted into the Laws of Arms. It is, therefore, very important to realise that the commentary of Rosehaugh is not only on the Act of 1592 but it reflects practices which were still in existence under that act in the seventeenth century, and not those which have prevailed subsequently to the passing of the 1672 Act. It refers, as a consequence, to an

---

[1] *Ut supra*, p. 11.

[2] It seems quite clear from the internal evidence of the book that it was written *before* 1672, and then partially revised, with some inserts after 1672, and published in 1680. The unwary reader would assume from the date 1680 that the book had been written in the light of the 1672 Act of Parliament, whereas it was written before it. Consequently Rosehaugh quotes here the 1592 Act and not that of 1672.

intermediate state between that in which only the pre-existing nobility had a right to arms from Lyon, and that which now prevails.

The reason why Lyon under the 1592 Act, and prior to that of 1672, could not grant arms to non-nobles was because by doing so he would have automatically made them nobles, as arms were the insignia of nobility in Scotland. The recording of arms was an investiture in nobility. The reason why Lyon's authority as at 1592 was circumscribed in this direction is because at that stage (as in so many other matters of government) certain acts were reserved to the Sovereign alone.. At that time no lords of Council in any realm could, as the present Prime Minister does, select the names of certain persons and request the Sovereign to make them lords, knowing the Sovereign will in effect obey the wishes of the first minister. Such authority had not been delegated to other parties. Likewise, the Prince at that time still kept within his own hands, not only in Scotland, but in most other countries, the ennoblement of plebeians, and then either gave them their arms himself, without consulting his officers of arms, or did so in consultation with his King of Arms, or else he sent them to that officer to receive arms. While ever, therefore, the Prince exercised such functions under his own hands, the authority and scope of activity of the Kings of Arms was definitely circumscribed.[1]

In many countries, there developed in the course of the Middle Ages the concept of a patent of nobility to be accompanied or followed by that of the arms, which were the insignia of that nobility, and without which the nobility did not and could not function, either on field of battle, in court, or in legal matters. In such countries, especially of Western Europe, *the evidence of having arms was proof of being noble*, since at that stage the heralds could only allow arms to existing ancient nobility, or those ennobled persons sent to them by the Sovereign for

[1] The case which has been cited, that the Burgundian King of Arms could only grant arms to deserving persons, while Philippe le Beau reserved to himself the granting of Noblesse (according to Vienna MS. 7223) is probably explicable in the light of this principle which we see in Scotland. Virtuous and deserving persons were probably originally those recognised as having a right to arms because of their nobility. The Prince only at that stage could make Nobles. Later the concept of deserving persons was extended as we shall see, and with it the power of the King of Arms grew. We doubt very much whether this instance proves, what those who put it forward hope it does, that the granting of noblesse and arms are absolutely distinct functions.

arms. Nobility, strictly speaking, was still no evidence of possession of arms, and it could, therefore, exist without them. In view of the history we have seen of the growth of the noble caste over Europe before arms existed this is understandable. Consequently, the prince had to make the aspirant noble (so that he could join that society) before he came under armorial authority. Armenian nobility to this day is, generally speaking, without arms, and when some of them make matches with established nobility in Europe it is necessary for them to receive arms, and for Orders of Chivalry in their case to accept their standing of nobility on other grounds than the evidence of arms. But armorial honours where they were of recognised use in relation to nobility in Western Europe were evidence of being noble.[1]

That arms were restricted in the sixteenth century (the time of the Act of 1592) and up to the time Mackenzie of Rosehaugh wrote, which was some time before that of 1672, in many countries of Western Europe, to nobles and patricians generally is most emphatically stated by him more than once. Some of his statements we have already seen. Nowhere is this so clearly put as at the point where, after commenting on the controversy on prescription, and the opposing views of Bartolus and Tiraquel, he says—" But to quiet all debate in this controversie, *most of Nations have discharg'd the carrying of Arms to any, save Gentlemen, or such who have a special warrand* ". (That is those who are of *ancient* nobility, or those who are ennobled by a special warrant.) Elsewhere, he also says—" Heraldry is that Science, which teacheth us to give or know Arms " and " Arms may be defin'd to be Marks of hereditary honour, given or authorised by some Supreem Power, to gratify the Bearer, or distinguish Families ", and, later on he tells us that some authorities call arms *Tesserae Gentilitae* " and in the Civil Law they are called, Tituli ", adding still further that arms " let us know, if the Bearers be Noblemen or Gentlemen ".[2]

---

[1] This situation is what we find in Scotland, England and Ireland, and certain other realms of Western Europe. There were, however, exceptions where these remarks have to be qualified, as we shall see later, when we come to discuss the Empire and Hungary. Here, arising from the two-fold factors, first of powerful municipalities within the realms, and secondly of the realms lying, in part, outside the ambient of Nordic conquests, differences of development arose in some respects. These we shall discuss later.

[2] *Op. cit.*, p. 1.

If we turn to the *Statute of Milan*, in the Kingdom of Lombardy, which covers the acts ranging from those of Philip II of Austria in 1609 through to the Sovereign Ordinance of Empress Maria Theresa of Austria in 1767 setting up the *Heraldic Court of Milan*, all of which were codified in the Organic Laws on nobility in Lombardy in 1769, we find listed the persons who can be considered nobles, followed by the section on *Arms of Gentry and their Ornaments*, the opening of which states emphatically—*that no one in the Austrian Lombardy is permitted to use arms of gentry . . . in public, private or in the Church, on sepulchres, at funerals, on seals etc., etc., unless he is veritably a noble,* etc. as set out in the previous section of the Act. Later it goes on to draw attention to the necessity of registration with the King of Arms.[1]

From this it will be seen that exactly the same principles were obtaining in Lombardy at this time, the seventeenth to the eighteenth centuries, as we find laid down by the Lord Advocate, writing in the seventeenth with a background of sixteenth century legislation and authorities before him.

We shall see the same ideas reflected in English heraldic pronouncements at this period. Consequently the views of Sir George Mackenzie of Rosehaugh cannot in any way be taken as based upon the practice of the Kingdom of Scotland only.

If we turn to Austria, whose influence was being felt in Lombardy, we find that whatever may have been the tendency at some times to allow arms to non-nobles without nobilitation, there are a series of ordinances all through the seventeenth and eighteenth centuries forbidding, or at least restricting arms, in some way or another to non-nobles. There are the ordinances of 1st March 1664, 19th January 1667, 2nd February 1707, 12th September 1721, and 7th October 1736 which interdicted non-nobles (except with a special concession) from bearing helmets and coronets. In that of the 28th September 1765 the carrying of noble arms and styles was forbidden, while the Emperor Francis I, on the 15th February 1805, forbade non-nobles the use of arms without authority. By a decision of 7th August 1820 any question of conceding arms to burghers was disallowed, while the forbidding of the carrying of shields with helmets or coronets was again restated

---

[1] G. Degli Azzi and G. Cecchini, *Codice Nobiliare Araldico*, Florence, 1928, pp. 98-99.

in 1883:[1] From this it will be seen that even in a Germanic realm which had been by English and Scottish, and other standards, often quite lax, or at least prepared to concede arms without nobility from time to time, all through the period we have recited there was first of all a tightening up of the law, and a refusal to imagine anything as arms which was not ensigned of a helmet or coronet. In fact if an achievement was not *mit Schild und Helm*, it was considered no coat of arms at all, and if it was so ensigned it was noble, or at least patrician.

Only in the case of ecclesiastics were arms freely allowed, and this is because Churchmen have always been considered in most if not all realms noble by office, and so far as Austria was concerned, and several other Roman Catholic realms, the right of prescription was, and still is, accorded to Churchmen.

Portugal is an important continental country for the purpose of comparison with British armorial conceptions, owing to the long alliance which has subsisted between that country and England. It is of interest therefore to find that under Alphonso V, in 1466, plebeians were forbidden to bear arms in which the metals appeared. This was because devices in colour on colour were contrary to the law of arms and the authorities were not prepared to consider them arms at all: evidently they were to be regarded rather as a species of merchants' marks. In the next generation King Emmanuel reiterated this regulation and ordered all the arms of gentlemen of coat armour to be matriculated. While as late as 1807 the law was re-enacted which made it obligatory not to bear arms unless they had been matriculated or granted by the Crown.[2]

In Savoy, which lay closer to the practice of the British Isles than that of Austria, and which has influenced later Italian heraldry considerably, we find that the interpretation of the status of arms was very strict. Non-nobles were not permitted, in the reign of Amedeus VIII, by his statute of 1430, to bear arms at all. In 1597, the Duchess of Savoy (Catherine of Austria) forbade the use of arms without authority, while the prohibition was renewed by Charles Emmanuel

---

[1] Paul Adam, *De l'Acquisition et du Port des Armoires, Recueil du IV* Congrès International des Sciences Généalogique et Héraldique*, Brussels, 1958, pp. 99-100.

[2] Conte de São Payo, *Do directo heraldico Portuguès*, 1927.

in 1598.   In 1634 the prohibitions were repeated, with, however, the
right to establish arms on 60 years of peaceful and acknowledged use
of the arms.[1]   (The House of Savoy, as Kings of Italy, repeated their
interdict of the use of arms by non-nobles as late as 1929.[2])

Because arms were so generally regarded as the proof of nobility
in Western Europe and, as we shall show later, and have already
done in *Heraldic Cadency*,[3] heraldry was a universal system within that
part of Europe dominated by the feudal system, they became known
as *tesserae nobilitatis*.[4]   Therefore, returning to a consideration of Scottish
heraldry, it is clear that it is in that sense that arms as then understood
must be regarded.

At first sight the limitations upon the Kings of Arms at this stage
of the development of heraldic jurisdiction would seem to have rigidly
excluded them from granting arms to non-nobles.   But, as time passed
it is clear that exceptions were made, as the idea of what was noble
was enlarged.   It is quite evident that very early other conceptions
began to develop than those which restricted all government to the
descendants of the Germanic conquerors of many European lands.
For, equally with this socio-ethnological caste system over all Western
and Central Europe there existed the influence of Christianity.   The
Church had grown powerful, and claimed for itself certain rights and
privileges in the temporal as well as in its own spiritual sphere.   It laid
emphasis on other virtues than those merely associated with conquest
and secular legislation, such as upon the rule of law, the value of education, and the virtues of helping the weak.

Consequently, as the Middle Ages proper disintegrated, and the
Renaissance advanced, lawyers began to have a considerable influence
in the definition of what was and was not noble.   Sir George Mackenzie
is only summing up in the late seventeenth century what had already
become accepted as axiomatic for some couple of centuries, when he
discusses to whom Lyon might grant arms.   After pointing out that

[1] Paul Adam, *ut supra*, p. 100.

[2] Conte Zeininger de Borja, *Rivista Araldica*, 1949, p. 306 and again later in the legislation
of 1943, says only noble arms and established arms of distinct civility are recognised.   See
Bolletino Officiale de Corpo della Nobiltà Italiano.   Anno 1 No. 1.   June 1958.   Naples.

[3] Faber and Faber, London, 1961.

[4] Called by Alex. Nisbet, *System of Heraldry*, 1722, Vol. I, p. 3, *indiciae of noblesse*.

his Patent gave him power to grant to virtuous and worthy Persons, and did not allow him to grant arms to those not worthy to bear them, he went on to discuss those things which *nobilitate*.

In other words we have here, under the influence of the civil law and the Church, the development of the idea that besides those who are noble by right of *birth*, others may be noble by right of *office*. It follows, therefore, from this that although in the earlier times Lyon might not grant to any but those who were of the nobility of blood, that is gentry, and those who were by the Prince specifically ennobled, this latter class was now being extended to include those who had become noble by office, and so came under his jurisdiction. The argument appears to have run, if not stated so specifically, that if the Prince allowed a person to occupy a noble office, it was like another becoming possessed of a noble fief, and so it put him in the noble class, although it only made him noble for the space of his enjoyment of that office, and in that respect differed from an actual patent of ennoblement. If, therefore, certain people were temporarily noble they came within Lyon's jurisdiction, and he could grant them arms, which were the symbols of office of nobility. Since, however, Lyon knew no such thing as a grant of arms for *life*, then it followed from this that these arms, *tesserae nobilitatis*, were hereditary. Thus it came about that the grant of the arms confirmed not only the *de facto* personal nobility of the grantee, but conferred an hereditary nobilitation without that patent which in some realms was altogether indispensable.

This concept led to the necessity to define very rigidly what offices actually carried nobilitation with them, and Rosehaugh discussed what did and did not, as follows—First of all riches, as such, did not *nobilitate*.[1] Herein we get the stark contrast between the ideas of the civilisation which was rooted in a noble Europe and those which prevail today in a democratic society. Today, in a democracy, wealth is the surest foundation for getting the highest honours in the state. Through it office in parliament and government, to seats among the peers, are certainly more easily if not largely obtained. The receiving of the numerous " honours " handed out regularly " for public and political services " and on other causes tend to follow wealth. The

[1] *The Science of Heraldry*, Edinburgh, 1680, pp. 13 ff.

granting of such distinctions in earlier times would have been considered incompatible with the ideas of nobiliary law. To grant a man a knighthood for being the head of a great industrial concern, or for being a trade union secretary, would have been considered outrageous, and contrary to the best interests of society and the realm. For nobiliary distinctions were not to be given to people just because they had amassed to themselves wealth or industrial, commercial or similar power.

Although the possession of a noble fief was essential at some stage or another to every noble family, the mere acquirement of land did not nobilitate in all cases, no matter how considerable the property, for, as Mackenzie goes on to say " for else a Rich man might Ennoble himself : but these *feuda* [feus or fiefs] only render the possessors Noble, which are bestowed by the Prince, or confirmed by him. For a *few* [feu] in either of these cases make the receivers Noble, seeing the Prince is the Fountain of Honour ".[1]   Arnone, as we shall have cause to point out again, says the same thing : a title can only be taken from land where the new lord is noble, as gentility cannot be bought.[2]

It is of interest that the process which has been one of the most common for the *new men* in England to gain the attributes of gentility since the Tudor period, namely to move from the banking house, or merchant's warehouse, to a country estate, to become allegedly " county ", under the older regime would not have conferred the *cachet* which the possession of the country estate in fact does give in England to this very day.

Having thus dealt with the limitations of wealth and broad acres to nobilitate,[3] and for the mere possession of which the King of Arms would not be entitled to grant arms [4] on the score that the petitioners had become noble by occupation, Rosehaugh goes on to discuss what functions performed in the state did give life-nobility and so brought the persons concerned within the King of Arms' writ.

[1] *Op. cit.*, p. 13.

[2] Arnone, *Diritto Nobiliare Italiano, Storia ed Ordinamento*, Milano, 1935, p. 16.

[3] *The Science of Heraldry, op. cit.*, p. 13.

[4] This is no contradiction to the known fact that every acquirer of a landed estate could receive a coat of arms, since feus of that sort could at first only normally be purchased by those already noble.

He says[1] " The employment of a Souldier doth enoble, if it be honoured with any considerable command ".   Originally no one could be an officer who was not a gentleman.   The hangover from this conception is that of the " officer and gentleman " which is still part of the British military code.   It is not merely necessary to offend as an officer, to receive punishment from the Courts Martial, *but as a gentleman also*.   For a commissioned officer is, temporarily, noble by reason of his Commission, but he is no longer necessarily a gentleman by race.

Besides the armed services, we learn that " Church-Employments do nobilitate . . . And generally, it is a Law in Heraldry, that Doctors, Orators and Lawreat Poets may be honoured with Coats of Arms . . . and Vaschal. pag. 712 warrands this by a decision of the Courts of France ".

In France from 1641 till the Revolution the family of d'Hozier were hereditary Judges of Arms, and during their time of administration there was built up an elaboration of the jurisprudence on the right to arms.   This, in brief, laid it down that the classes entitled to arms were the *Nobility* : the titled to have the right to their coronet of rank over their arms, and the untitled to have a helmet with silver bars surmounting the shield.   *In addition*, those formerly not noble[2] who, by their services or the offices they held, had come to enjoy a nobility of calling which entitled them to arms.   These included general officers on land or sea ; titulars of noble offices ; lawyers such as magistrates of the Sovereign's Courts ; civil lieutenant generals ; mayors of towns ; burghers of Paris (with their helm in profile) in virtue of an erroneous, but traditional, interpretation of the privileges accorded to them by Charles V in 1371 ; officers of French and foreign orders of chivalry ; and all who had concessions from the King.   These could bear their arms with the additaments such as those to which the established nobility were entitled.   Besides these there were others who could petition for arms and these included : priests ; people of plebeian origin *who possessed noble fiefs* (who were thus ennobled by their fiefs) ; subalterns of the army ; officers of the judicature who

---

[1] *Op. cit.*, p. 14.

[2] Paul Adam, *De l'Acquisition et du port des Armoires, Recueil du IVe Congrès international des Sciences Généalogique et Héraldique*, Brussels, 1958, p. 91.

were not of a sovereign court ; and burghers who were living nobly.[1]
The latter being equivalent to what in England was considered a
qualification for consideration, namely living in such a manner as they
had the port of gentry—and somewhat analogous to the Italian category
of *distinct civility*.

The learned professions, the universities and the Church are thus
all of them noble occupations, and their members temporarily noble.
An aspect of this is seen in the fact that to this day in the Church of
Rome all parish priests need to have arms if they strictly carry out the
customs of the Church, and in Lyon Court to this day also, a Church-
man is always treated as noble in his own person.

This view was universal, and not limited to English, Scottish and
French heralds and jurists, and so we find Salvioli reflecting the same
view from Italian sources, where, in his treatise on heraldry, he summarises the various degrees of nobility, such as those of race from
ancient times, and those who have gained it in the court, in council
and by arms, and the nobility of the toga, being a nobility conferred
on the soldiers of science, medical doctors, advocates in law, magistrates,
and so forth.[2]

It will be observed that the emphasis is altogether different from
that of the present age. We pretend that the persons being honoured
have deserved well of the state, but the measure of how we estimate
their deserving is more often than not the measure of how well they
have done for themselves. The greater the economic, industrial or
other power they wield, the greater their possessions, the more sure
they are of respect and advancement—whereas, at the other extreme,
the village parson, the city priest, the university lecturer, the man
of letters, unless they are writing best-sellers and so worthy of adulation,
are treated with tolerant condescension by those who would have
themselves been disqualified from consideration for any advancement
at all in the age of chivalry. Service to the community and the state
as a whole was the key-stone for personal honour, and not service to
oneself.

The Civil Law (to which the Law of Arms belongs) was, of course,

---

[1] Paul Adam, *ut supra*, p. 91.
[2] 9th Edition, Turin, 1930, p. 313.

not entirely unrealistic. It appreciated that wealth was desirable (where possible) for the maintenance of the social position of nobility, and that " nobility is nothing oftimes but ancient riches ".[1] But, with all that it was nevertheless held, as we have seen, that wealth was not the foundation of nobility, and, what is more, nobility could survive without it.

The influence of wealth was considered to have a bearing solely in controlling *the rank within the nobility*, for, obviously, an earl, marquis, or duke, who was poorer than a country gentle-man was an anachronism, and unable, because of his poverty, to discharge the great duties attached to his rank. Consequently, because, " Nobility being a right derived from Blood, it seems to have no Dependence upon Riches ",[2] as was expressly stated in Roman law, a noble could only be downgraded in nobiliary *rank*— and then it needed a special act of parliament to do it. This we find was the case in the degradation of rank for this cause of George Neville, Duke of Bedford in the time of Edward IV of England. Commenting upon which Sir George Mackenzie of Rosehaugh says—

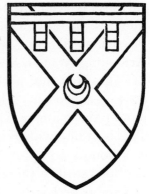

George Neville, Duke of Bedford temp. Edw. IV

> " though a person who is noble by Birth should fall into poverty, yet that poverty can no more Degrade him from his Nobility, then it can taint his Blood ; but though it cannot root out that Noble Character from his Blood, and make him no Gentleman, yet it seems a good reason why he may be Degraded from being a Peer of the Realm : For the being a Peer is no necessar[y] effect of Blood, but a mark of the Royal bounty, bestowed for the better Government and Advantage of the Kingdom ".[3]

It is a natural outcome of this way of thinking that the late medi-aeval and renaissance heralds should have gone on to consider by what means nobility could be lost. This was a logical corollary—for if nobility could be acquired by the grade and rank of the profession

[1] Mackenzie of Rosehaugh, *op. cit.*, p. 13.

[2] Mackenzie of Rosehaugh, *Observations upon the Laws and Customs of Nations, as to Precedency*, Edinburgh, 1960, p. 81.

[3] *Ut supra.*

which was exercised, so could it be lost also by the same principles. In this we have again a stark contrast from the conditions and standards of a capitalist society. Mackenzie states nobility " is not lost by poverty, even in the longest course of time, *Tiraquel, cap. 5* ". Furthermore it is not lost " by exercising mean trades . . . But when they leave off these, they return to their former Dignities . . . But being an Advocat is accounted no such Trade . . . And therefore in France, they, as all other Gentlemen, are exempted from paying taxes . . . Physicians likewise, and their posterity have a right to bear Coat-Armours, *Tiraquel, cap. 31* ".[1]

Thus it is that a nobleman does not lose his nobility by having to have recourse to inferior employment, except, presumably, in a temporary manner when it would bring his nobility into contempt. This is in line with English law which laid it down that if a gentleman was bound an apprentice to a merchant or other trade he did not lose his gentility thereby : but a man who was noble by office lost it as soon as he lost his office.[2]

Concerning merchants, which term includes what we would call also bankers, and stockbrokers, and the rest, we read that though "most worthy members of the Commonwealths, yet they are not noble nor Gentlemen by their profession . . . nor should they have Coat-Armours ; but the Laws of Heraldry, and the general custom of the World allows them a Merchants mark ".[3]

The intense dislike of the whole of the mediaeval, and later, world for the man who bought, sold, haggled and, as they deemed it, took unfair advantage of another, and made money his main aim in life, is very foreign to us, and difficult for our civilisation to understand. These few brief quotations from Sir George Mackenzie give some appreciation of these concepts as they came to be encased in the law by the late renaissance period and into the seventeenth century.

In view of the fact that a peer could be degraded for lack of means to maintain his estate, and that even nobility was suspendable during the exercise of mean trades, we may remark, incidentally, that it

---

[1] *The Science of Heraldry*, Edinburgh, 1680, p. 14.
[2] Hugh Clark, *An Introduction to Heraldry.* London, 1859. 16th Edition, p. 241.
[3] Sir George Mackenzie, *The Science of Heraldry, op. cit.*, pp. 14-15.

would have gone hard with many peers today. For if common news-paper reports are true, in their own persons and those of their families some of them run tea rooms, serve as tapsters or strum instruments in public houses, and in other ways bring their titles and ranks into con-tempt. Such conduct would have been held to be derogatory to nobility in an earlier age. They would certainly have been deprived of their peerages, and all the status which stems from them, saving only their basic nobility, of which they cannot be deprived. Even that, however, would have been lost to some of them, for being tapsters and the like, while ever they occupied themselves in these trades. If sheer necessity had forced any noble, and certainly a peer, to become a tapster, he would then have been expected to have hidden his identity. Today some of them flout it to the world, to gain more notoriety and " custom " for themselves, and actually seek to make money out of their rank. This is wholly at variance with the concepts of nobiliary law, under which a noble is to serve and give to the community, and not exploit it by using titles, designation of rank and gentility as a means for personal advantage. Nothing probably is more contempt-ible than an " honourable " or lord caterwauling " hill-billy " songs for gain. On the other hand when after the collapse of the family of Winslade, at the end of the disastrous Wars of the Roses, the last heir of that line was compelled, through sheer necessity, to go from one mansion house to another with his harp, he did not lose his nobility, as he performed a noble act in a seemly manner, to his own kind, and the whole Duchy of Cornwall felt pity (not contempt) to see a gentle-man of ancient name brought so low.

However, nobiliary law did and does not, preclude a noble from earning his living and there is no basis of justification for the type, sheltering behind gentility, which would rather be idle than work. The law was only concerned as to *how* a man earned his living. It had to be in a calling which was not only honourable in status, but one which did not produce a meanness of spirit and outlook. To be a money-lender would be dishonourable for a noble, to be forced to be a clerk would not be.

It is, therefore, quite certain that at the end of the Middle Ages the legalistic concept of the term noble had begun to be extended to those who held noble offices, and performed noble tasks, such as those of magistrates and the rest. They became, as a consequence, automatically under the authority of the King of Arms and could receive arms. By this means there was transmitted the personal nobility from the temporary offices of the grantees to all their descendants. It will be seen from the reference above to the physicians that it would appear that the idea had already taken root to some extent that even this nobility of a temporary nature had begun to transmit itself to the descendants, so that they too could be the recipients of arms.

It will be evident that this legalistic interpretation of the position (which is to be expected from an erudite Lord Advocate, skilled in the Civil Law of which the Law of Arms is a part, with a considerable knowledge of the legal systems of the Continent) reaches the same conclusion as the English heraldic writers of the period. " For they conclude that the King of Arms could grant to anyone having the " port of a gentleman ". In other words if he had reached a noble position in the estimation of society he was entitled to sue for arms, to give legal expression to the *de facto* status he had reached.

It follows from this that most of those very people who, at an earlier period, would have been just the persons to whom the Prince would have given Patents of Nobility, on the basis of which they would have received arms, were now tacitly accepted as noble in their persons by their offices. The need, therefore, for the Prince to confer patents of nobility became much less frequent. Consequently, in both England and Scotland it seems quite evident, in contrast with what happened in some other realms, the direct ennoblement by the Prince himself ceased, and fell into desuetude. The powers of the Kings of Arms became extended to granting arms to people who had reached the status of nobility by the customs of the realms concerned, and so it fell to them to confer the *tesserae nobilitatis*.

Thus, what it was said at first the King of Arms had not power to do —which was to ennoble—in fact he came to do by his grants becoming the device of confirming and making hereditary the personal nobility which had been achieved by the petitioners. This change is reflected in the difference between the Act of 1592 and that of 1672 of the Scottish Parliament. The former is taken up with matriculating arms to established nobles, but the second and later act also adds that Lyon " may give Armes to vertuous and well-deserving Persones ". Thus the *tesserae nobilitatis* can be conferred, on Lyon's own authority, to virtuous and well-deserving persons, such as the classes we have been discussing. By this step in the extension of his power, the King of Arms thus relieved the Prince of the need to issue personally patents of nobility, and he became his Commissioner for Nobility.

Furthermore, it cannot be argued that such arms were not noble since, in the same century, The Act in Favour of the Lyon King of Arms against Painters, Goldsmiths and Others [1] clearly says—" such persons as are not privileged by the law of arms or by warrant from His Majesty to wear coat armour or *cognissance of gentry* ". This makes it clear that arms were still regarded as *tesserae nobilitatis*.

Edmondson

We have thus followed through, in the procedure of the Scottish Court of Chivalry, clear evidence of the evolution of the powers of the Kings of Arms, from the stage at which they dealt solely with matriculations and confirmations of arms to established nobility, to that when they had added to their duties grants to those ennobled by the Prince, and finally to the stage at which all those who were by office held to be noble could receive permanent ensigns of nobility not only for themselves but also for transmission to their descendants. Since the Court of the Lord Lyon functions under these very same acts which we have mentioned, and has done so without interruption since the times with which we have been dealing, it is unquestionably still the law in Scotland that arms are cognizances of nobility.

It might be as well to observe that there has been a complete continuity of opinion on the part of heraldic authorities in Scotland from the sixteenth and seventeenth centuries to the present in support of these conclusions. Space will not permit extensive quotation. But since, in a succeeding chapter, we shall be citing the considerable authority of the eighteenth century English Herald, Edmondson, it

[1] Innes of Learney, *Scots Heraldry*, Oliver & Boyd, Edinburgh, 1956, pp. 244 ff.

D

might be as well to add here the no less authoritative Scottish authority of the same period, Nisbet, 1742, who says most explicitly—

> Arms are hereditary Marks of Honour . . . granted or authorised by Sovereigns for distinguishing, differencing, and illustrating Persons, Families and Communities. . . . From these Definitions the Use of Arms is obvious, viz. . . . to distinguish and Difference Persons, Families and Communities : so as . . . *to distinguish the Nobility and Gentry from the Vulgar* . . . As to the First of these Uses, viz. *The Distinction of the Nobility from the Vulgar*, it is plain from the aforesaid Definition, that no Person or Family are entitled to carry Arms, but such as have received, or assumed the same by approbation of Sovereign Authority, *which is sufficient to distinguish* the Vulgar from the Nobility and Gentry.[1]

Therefore, whatever may be the position of arms furth of Scotland, there is no doubt that in Scotland their possession constituted,

Fox-Davies

and still does constitute, the same thing as evidence of nobility elsewhere. We do not think that this is just a peculiar nobiliary evolution restricted to Scotland alone. We shall shortly proceed to consider the evidence from English heraldic procedure, where we shall find confirmation of this point of view, as we shall when we go farther afield. But nowhere is the law so specific on the matter as it is in Scotland, and consequently it has been desirable to consider the evolution of this development as it occurred in that realm first. We are well aware that there is a school of thought which denies the fact that English heralds have the power to ennoble by grant of arms. All we would say is that if the evidence from English heraldic law is consistent with the very clear law on the subject from Scotland then it is certain whatever *lacunae* may have existed in English pronouncements on occasions, that it can only be interpreted in the light of the Scottish administration of the Law of Arms. We would also add that it would be a matter of great surprise if two realms, in the same island, sharing so much the same currents of life, should have evolved diametrically opposite values for coats of arms. The onus certainly rests with those who

---

[1] Alexander Nisbet, Gent., *A System of Heraldry, Speculative and Practical*, Edinburgh, 1742.

oppose, as a residue from the former cross-purpose-controversies, as Dr. Wagner rightly calls them,[1] between Oswald Barron and A. C. Fox-Davies, this interpretation of the Law of Arms. It lies with them to prove that an English patent for a coat of arms was not a symbol of investiture of nobility. However, we shall shortly return to this subject when we come to examine the English administration of the Law of Arms at this period down to the present time.

[1] Anthony R. Wagner, *Heraldry in England*, The King Penguin Books, 1946, p. 24.

CHAPTER IV

THE NOBILIARY STATUS OF ARMS IN ENGLAND FROM THE 15th TO THE 18th CENTURIES

THUS far we have followed the principles of Scottish Law, not only as a means of understanding what is the Scottish Law of Arms, but also as a key to that of England and other realms sharing wholly, or mainly, the same nobiliary law.

The corner stone upon which Scottish heraldic law is seen to rest is upon the fact that arms are evidence of noblesse, and that they are feudalised heritage which has a nobiliary value. We believe that when we review the principles of English heraldic law, as it emerges in the following pages, it will be found difficult to escape the conclusion that in all essentials it does not differ materially from that of Scotland with which we have just been dealing. With that end in view we will examine the nobiliary principles which it seems evident to us form the foundation of English heraldry and its administration by the English officers of arms.

The distinguished English herald, Edmondson, in his book—*A Complete Body of Heraldry*, 1780—says that, in the Commissions by the Sovereign to the English Kings of Arms in the Tudor period, and on down to later times also, " these commissions enjoined all . . . not to call, name, or write, in any assize, session, court or other place, or give in any writing the addition of Esquire or Gentleman to or for any person whatsoever, unless he was able to stand unto or *justify the same by the law of arms* ". This view is supported by the statement of John Bossewell, gentleman, writing in 1572, in his *Workes of Armorie* (Fol. I)

¹ Vol. I, p. 159.

where he says of arms that these are " signs and tokens of honor, which commonly of Heraultes be called Armes, or Badges of gentlemen. They bee also called *Symbola heroica*, signes, prices [prizes], or markes appertainying to noblenesse : and whereby every estate, or man of great aucthoritie is knowne : the noble from the ignoble, the gentle from the ungentle : and the free man from the bond ". While Sir John Ferne, in his *Glory of Generosity*, 1573, says " Any man may give away his estate to a stranger ; *but his* Arms, the Ensigns of his Nobility, he cannot". It should be noted that Ferne is quoted elsewhere [1] by Selden [2] who tells us that in the tournaments the opening proclamations began with " Heare you this my Lordes, all true knights and Gentlemen bearers of armes ", etc.

Bossewell

Selden goes on to discuss single combat in the duel to settle differences over coat-armour, and says " Our division hath this other part of trials of private rights and interests, which are either touching Gentry and bearing of coat-armour ", etc. After citing [3] such trials over coats of arms he says—" Examples of such titles to ensignes of Nobility tried by proofe on body are that of Sir John Chandos, an English knight, and the Lord del Cleremont a Frenchman ", etc.

The Boke of St. Albans, another early authority, has such a statement which clearly relates gentry to arms as—" How gentlemen be made that be not of coat armour nor blood ".   The same writer says elsewhere, " And yet the Kyng shall nott make a knyght with owte a coat of arms byfore ". This means that since knights were made from esquires, all esquires had to have arms. In other words, they were nobles. [4]

[1] *Lib. de Glor. nobil.*, p. 327.
[2] John Selden, *The Duello*, or *Single Combat*, London, 1610, p. 44.
[3] John Selden, *op. cit.*, p. 47.
[4] *The Boke of St. Albans* elsewhere says that if a Sovereign King makes a yeoman a knight he becomes a nobleman by the royalty of the king and of knighthood. But, if no inconsistency is inferred between the two passages, it is to be assumed that the knighthood is preceded by the taking of arms, wherein lies the nobility, but the arms, in this case, could not have been taken had it not been for the purpose of being knighted.

Elsewhere, *The Boke of St. Albans*,[1] speaking of the conditions for acceptance into the Order of St. Lazarus at that time, says—" before they enter into this knighthood (he) must prove himself to bee born in lawfull wedlocke, and a Gentleman both by father and mother, and to beare Armes . . . that he and his ancestors haue eueer liued as Gentleman, without use of any base or mecanical occupation ".

Richard Jhones,[2] another sixteenth century writer, speaks of " what pedigree, Armes, or badges soever are to warrant their antiquities or nobilitie ".

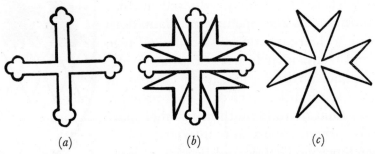

(a)   (b)   (c)

Badge of the Order of SS. Maurice and Lazarus (*b*) and those of St. Maurice (*a*) and St. Lazarus (*c*)

It is clear from all these writers, covering the sixteenth century and into the eighteenth, that arms are taken unquestionably as insignia of nobility or gentility. It cannot be construed that these writers only mean that these arm display the particular gentility of certain individual families, while *all* arms do not necessarily do so. If arms did not guarantee nobility there would have been no grounds for fighting duels over them. Neither would it have been necessary to show evidence of gentle ancestry by being armigerous. Had arms been permitted to simple as gentle then in proof of gentility there would have been no point in demanding proof of arms.

We have thus far been dealing with the opinions of learned writers. But we have evidence still extant from surviving legal documents which clearly prove that these views were well founded. Thus, if we take the

---

[1] *The Fifth Book*, p. 62, as printed in Dallaway.
[2] *The Booke of Honor and Armes*. Printed by Richard Jhones, London, 1590. Fourth Book, p. 52.

letters patent which are called either *of nobilitation*, or *grants of arms*, which are in the British Museum from the fifteenth century we find examples such as that of Henry VI, 1444, to Arnold and Grimond de

Burdeux   Richmond Clarenceux

Mattock   St. George

Bordeu,[1] which reads—" to which Arnold and Grimond and of those procreated of them, by our special grace we make and create nobles.[2] And in evidence of such nobility we give and concede by these presents and in these our letters patent the arms depicted. "

Or, again, if we take the Letters Patent of Richmond, Clarenceux

[1] Rymer 132 ; Harl. MS 1507, B.M.

[2] This answers completely those who say that noblesse has never existed in England as a status recognised by law, and that patents of nobility have never been issued. This is a grant of arms, but it is as clearly a grant of nobility.

King of Arms,[1] in the ninth year of Henry VII (1494), the beginning
of the Tudor period, we read—

> " I the said king of arms, not only by common renown, but also by my own
> knowledge, and report of many other credible and noble persons, verily
> ascertained that Nicholas Mattok of Hitchin in the County of Hertford hath
> well and honorably guided and governed himself, so that he hath deserved
> and is right worthy, he and his posterity, to be in all places of worship,
> admitted, renowned, accounted, numbered, accepted, and received, unto the
> number and into the company of our ancient gentles and noble men per-
> petually from henceforth; and for remembrance and consideration of the
> same his gentleness, virtue, and ability, by the authority and power of my
> office, I the said king of arms have devised, ordained, and assigned unto and
> for the same Nicholas and for his posterity the arms here following " etc. etc.

Taking these two documents together we see in the first the Prince
giving letters patent himself to the ennobled and with them the arms.
A half-century later we find the king of arms himself (as the King's
Commissioner) granting the arms and nobility in the letters patent he
issues.[2]

By the time of Henry VIII we get references in his commissions
to his Kings of Arms to the use of the term *ennoblishing*, which makes
it clear that ennobling fell within their prerogatives. Thus in Henry
VIII's patent to Benolt Clarencieux, dated 19th April 1530 he says
that those who " by the service doon to US, or to other that be en-
creased or augmentid to possessions and riches hable to maynteyne
the same . . . all such as shall be *enoblished* to have their armes regestred
in the Erle Marshalles boke ".[3]

The practice of the English heralds at the time of the Visitations
(which lasted until the end of the seventeenth century) is entirely
consistent with these interpretations of the significance of arms. Thus

[1] Harl. MS. 1507, B.M.

[2] When the king only granted arms it was believed that the King of Arms had no higher
authority to do so above that which already resided in any nobleman by prescriptive right.
This is clear from the *Boke of St. Albans* where we read—" And it is the opynyon of moni men
that an herrod armis may gyve arms. Bot I say if any sych armys be borne by any herrod
given that thoos armys be of no more auctorite then thoos armys the wich be take by a mannys
awne acutorite ". Here we see the stages in the development of the heralds' authority : first
only to record the grants the king made to nobles ; secondly to grant only to established
nobles ; and finally to grant arms and nobilitation as the Royal Commissioners.

[3] A. R. Wagner, *Heralds and Heraldry*, p. 9.

to take the example of the Visitation of Durham in 1615,[1] we read that Norroy King of Arms' warrant reads expressly as follows—

> These are to require you, and in the King's Majesty's Name, to charge and command you forthwith upon sight hereof, to warn those Knights, Esquires, and Gentlemen, whose names are underwritten, and all the rest within your Ward, *as well as those that assume the titles as others*, personally to appear before me, Richard St. George, Norroy King of Arms, on Thursday, being the twenty-fourth day of August next, at Widow Hudspithe's, in Clapitt Street, within the city of Duresme, (where I intend to sit, for the registering of the Knights, Esquires, and Gentlemen within your Ward) and that they bring with them such Arms and Crests as they now use and bear, with their Pedigrees and Descents, and such of their evidences and ancient writings, as if need require, may justify the same ; that I knowing how they use and challenge those titles and bear their arms, may make entrance of the same acordingly. But if I shall not hear from them upon this notice by you given, then these contempts will force me to proceed as my commission appointeth in such cases, not only to adjourn those that be Gentlemen to answer the same, before the Lords and Commissioners for the office of Earl Marshal of England, on a day prefixed, but also to disclaim and make infamous by proclamation *all such as shall refuse to make proof of their Gentry, having usurped the title thereof without just authority and just calling* . . .
>
> " My honourable good friends and neighbours, this is a service which concerneth your honours and arms, and the good of your posterity, and for the continuance and recording of your Gentrys and Pedigrees . . .

It will be observed that throughout this proclamation there is no suggestion that the proof of gentry lies in anything else besides proofs of descent, arms and crests.[2]

The English heralds were so earnest in their application of the Laws of Arms that not only did they record those who were claimants for recognition as gentry, but they equally disclaimed those who had usurped the rank of nobility. Edmondson[3] commenting on these disclaimers says—" Such persons as had usurped titles or dignities,

---

[1] J. Foster, *Pedigrees recorded at the Visitations of the County Palatine of Durham*, London, 1887, pp. 342-3.

[2] It should be observed that *Visitations* were not limited to England. In Piedmont, there was legislation starting with the *Statute of Savoy*, 1430, to control arms, with in 1613 a compilation of a special register, followed by, in 1687, the institution of *Visitations*. These Visitations were for the registration of arms of *families traditionally noble*. From this it is clear that there is a distinct relation between arms and nobility as in the case of the English Visitations.

[3] Edmondson, *A Complete Body of Heraldry*, 1780. Vol. I, p. 160.

or bore ensigns of gentility, which did not belong to them, were obliged, under their own hands, to disclaim all pretence or title there-unto for the future, and, for their presumption in having publicly used such titles and ensigns, without having any right thereto, were degraded by proclamations made by the common cryer, in the market-place of the town nearest to their usual place of abode ".

The proclamation of Disclaimed Persons in 1615 by Norroy King of Arms, in the Visitation of Durham which we have just cited, makes it clear beyond any shadow of doubt that the English heraldic law in no wise differed from the Laws of Arms as they were understood by Mackenzie of Rosehaugh, who based his conclusions upon the pro-cedures of the two realms with which he was well-acquainted—Scotland and France. For Norroy says—

> The King's most excellent Majestie being desirous that the Nobilitie [1] and Gentrie of this Realm should be preserved in everie degree, as well in honour as in worship, and that everie person and persons, bodies politique and corporate, and others, should be knowne in his estate, degree, and misteries, without confusion and discords, hathe authorised me . . . not only to visit all the sayd provence, to preserve, take knowledge, survey, and vewe all manner of arms, cognisances, creastes, and other like devices, with the notes of the descents, pedegrees, and mariages of all the Nobles and Gentrie therein throughout conteined, but also to reprouve, controul, and make infamous by proclamation, all such as unlawfully and without just authority, vocation, and due calling, doe or have done, or shall usurp and take upon him or them anie name or title of honor or dignitie, as Esquere, Gent. or others, as by His Highnes' gracious commission, under the Great Seal of England, more plainly may appear. Know ye therefore, that I, the said Richard St. George, Norroy, for the accomplishment of His Majestie's desire and further-ance of His Highnes' service that way, at this present makinge survey within the county of Duresme, found these persons, whose names are underwritten, presumptuously and without any good ground or authoritie to have usurped the names and titles of Gentlemen, contrarie to all right and to the ancient customes of this land *and the usage of the law of armes*, which name and title they are from henceforth no more to use nor take upon them, upon such further pains and penalties as by the Earl Marshall of England, or His Majestie's most honour-able Commissioners for the executing of the office of Earl Marshal, shall be inflicted and layd upon them . . .

---

[1] By this time the improper use of *nobility* for peerage had become established, and should be so understood in this context.

At the Visitation of Huntingdonshire, 1613,[1] we find the Lancaster Herald issuing proclamation to the effect that—

> I doe intend to sitt for the better registering of all the gentlemen within your Hundred, and to bringe with them such their armes and crests as they now use and beare, with their discents, pedigrees, and patentes of armes, and other their evidences as may justify the same if need require : to the intent that I, knowing how they use and challenge the names of esquires and gentle-men, and beare their coates of armes, may accordingly take notice thereof, and record the same, and to disclayme all those that falsely and without true ground have usurped or taken the title of esquires or gentlemen upon them.

The records of the English Court of Chivalry uphold completely this interpretation of the significance of the right to arms, as we shall

Baker

Coke

see presently in a succeeding chapter. All that is necessary here is to cite the case of W. Baker, gent., 21st November 1637. Because it has been well-cited elsewhere,[2] we need not give in full. The plaintiff complains he was abused and called " noe Gentleman ". Le Neve, Clarenceux King of Arms, was instructed to examine the point, and " having done so, declared as touching the gentry of William Baker, that Robert Cooke, Clarenceux King of Arms, did make a declaration 10th May 1573, under his hand and seals of office, that George Baker of London, sonne of J. Baker of the same place, sonne of Simon Baker of Faversham, co. Gent., *was a bearer of tokens of honour*, and did allow

---

[1] *The Visitation of the County of Huntingdon*, edited by Sir Henry Ellis, Camden Society, 1849, p. 137.

[2] A. C. Fox-Davies, *A Complete Guide to Heraldry*. Nelson, Edinburgh, 1950, p. 21.

and confirm to the said George Baker and to his posterity " etc. etc. From which it is clear that the Court regarded the tokens of honour (arms) as the salient evidence as to gentility.

Not only was such the finding of the competent English Court which was concerned with nobility, gentility and arms, but it was also the view held by the Common law of England, as we have the dictum of the great English lawyer Coke of the late Tudor and Jacobean periods (1552-1634)—*Nobiles sunt qui arma gentilicia antecessorum suorum proferre possunt.* (Those are Nobles who are able to put forward arms of gentility of their own ancestors.)

The tendency to a confused use of gentle and noble in early English writers (before noble meant peer) is due to the fact that at this period they were tending to think of the established nobility who were also gentry, and the two terms, although different, were largely interchangeable. The distinction only had to be drawn when newly created nobility had to be distinguished from established and old nobility, who were gentry. Hence in Coke's statement he talks of nobles having the arms of gentility. His meaning, however, is absolutely plain, in that he is making it categorically clear that those who are noble (or gentle) are those who have inherited arms. (In a succeeding chapter we shall deal fully with the precise definition of these nobiliary terms of noble and gentle.)

It may also be observed that the concepts which we have seen were accepted by the Scottish heralds concerning the non-noble character of trade, and the classes who could receive arms, were not restricted to them alone.

Echoes of these concepts we get in the statements of later English authorities. For instance, Edmondson[1] says that " our ancient [English] gentry . . . would not bear that any person among the lower class, although gotten rich, should use such tokens of gentilitial distinctions ". Arms were not only insignia of nobility, but they were denied by public opinion and custom to the self-made rich man, since, as Mackenzie of Rosehaugh stated in Scotland, riches cannot be allowed to nobilitate, and were not a score on which arms could be granted. The same concept comes out again where Edmondson tells us of the

[1] Edmondson, *A Complete Body of Heraldry*, Vol. I, p. 89.

reasons for the removal of Sir William Dethick from his office of Garter King of Arms in 1603—" He also in the same time, and long after, committed very many gross abuses, as namely the giving of arms, yea, and of some of the nobility, to base and ignoble persons ". Here we have the case of the King of Arms, as Commissioner for Nobility, transgressing his authority and giving arms to the new-rich, who had no claims, other than their riches, to consideration. In John Guillim's *A Display of Heraldrie* in 1660,[1] we see the further development of what offices were noble in themselves, and to the possessors of which the King of Arms could grant arms. For he says—that the military commanders and " skilful professors of the Civill Lawes . . . learned proficients, and the judicious students, in other Arts and Professions, might receive remuneration for their vertues " by grants of arms. Further he adds— " And without doubt there is great reason that Armes should be distributed unto men, renowned for their learning and wisdome, who with expence, even of their lives and spirits in

Guillim

continuall study, to enable themselves to be fit to serve the Wealpublick at home, by magistracy, and civill government, where they may no lesse merit reward of their Prince at home, by their Politick managing of civill affaires ; than the Martiall man abroad . . And this is the cause that Armes are given for remuneration in later times, as well to learned and religious men, as to Martiall men ".[2]

In Scottish heraldic practice we have the categoric authority of a series of Acts of Parliament, and the legal commentaries of Mackenzie of Rosehaugh, the Lord Advocate of Charles II, to underline and emphasise the interpretation of the Act of 1592, and international practice as it affected Scotland. From this we have been able to trace without any ambiguity the enlargement of the King of Arms' powers, and the broadening of the concepts of nobility, and those who, as nobles, could receive arms. It is now clear from these documents

[1] Pp. 10-11.
[2] John Guillim, *A Display of Heraldrie*, 4th Edition, London, 1660, p. 11.

we have now reviewed that English heraldry is absolutely parallel to that which we have studied in Scotland, down to and inclusive of the eighteenth century when Edmondson was writing.

Not only so, but in fact, English heraldry undoubtedly preceded Scottish heraldry in each one of these developments. For we find that Clarenceux was already granting arms and nobilitation by the end of the fifteenth century. This is not surprising since Scotland tended then, as now, to be slower than England to accept innovations. It was much more feudal (as it still remains). Furthermore, it had not experienced the decimation of its ancient nobility, which occurred in the English Wars of the Roses which ended with the death of Richard III in 1485 and which forced upon England a wholesale recruitment of new people to her nobility, and thus a flood of nobilitations to fill the gaps. Consequently, whereas in a normal, stable, feudal society nobilitations would be relatively few, controlled personally by the Prince, in England a situation must have arisen in which the King had to delegate his own powers of nobilitation to the Kings of Arms to relieve himself of the burden. In Scotland, with its nobility and feudal structure unimpaired, with strong resistance to the *new man*, the capitalist adventurer as he would be considered, the Prince had no need to delegate his powers of nobilitation so early. The Union of the Crowns, apart from the fashion which had grown up in England where the Kings of Arms were granting insignia of nobility over a wider class than to the established noblesse, must have been one of the principal reasons for accelerating the devolution of powers from the Crown to Lyon King of Arms—for once the King was located in London it simply was not practicable for him to control personally the nobilitation of new men by grants of arms. Hence this single event accounts for the fact that the act of 1672, after the Union of the Crowns, gives Lyon far more power than the act of 1592 which preceded the conjunction of the regal power of the two kingdoms.

It seems inescapable from what we have said that we can do no other than conclude that the Laws of Arms were exactly the same in both kingdoms at the periods we are discussing, from the Middle Ages till the early part of the eighteenth century. Therefore the qualities associated with arms in one kingdom are applicable to the other, any lacunae in the known practices of English heralds, through the absence of any statutes such as those under which the Scottish heralds function, can be justifiably filled by reference to Scottish practice under such statutes.

In support of this conclusion it may be further observed that when James VI and I came to the throne of England, he did not conceive of two distinctly different orders of nobles and society in his two kingdoms. His conception was that they were identical and equivalent in all their grades. It is, therefore, inconceivable that after two more generations of a common crown the Scottish Parliament could carry out legislation in 1672 which was in any single particular inconsistent with what was held to be the Law of Arms south of the Border.

James VI and I

In conclusion we might draw attention to the term sometimes met with at this stage in English heraldry, of the " port " of a gentleman, which is the criterion as to who could receive arms and who could not. We suggest that this has to be interpreted in the terms of the facts we have reviewed. A person who practised a noble occupation, or whose immediate ancestors had, and who lived in all other respects as a member of the noblesse would, had the " port of a gentleman " and so was entitled to sue for arms and nobilitation.[1]

---

[1] Later we shall show more exactly what was meant by this term, when we come to discuss the more precise meaning of *noble* and *gentle* respectively in relation to each other.

CHAPTER V

THE EVIDENCE OF THE ENGLISH COURT OF CHIVALRY IN THE 17th CENTURY CONCERNING THE SIGNIFICANCE OF ARMS

THANKS to the recent publications of Mr. G. D. Squibb, Q.C. there have been made available several monographs on the English Court of Chivalry—the Earl Marshal's Court, the records of which are clearly consistent with the Law of Arms as we have so far interpreted them from the Scottish and English sources which have been discussed.

The Court of Chivalry in England being, as elsewhere, a court of the Civil Law as distinct from the English Common Law, it did not rely upon case law until late in its history—indeed not till the end of the eighteenth century.[1] Consequently, this fact alone implies that the principles applied in other courts of chivalry, which were equally grounded on the Civil Law, must have been the basis of the law as exercised in the Earl Marshal's Court. This admission alone infers, therefore, that there could have been no fundamental difference between, say, the Lyon Court (the Court of Chivalry of Scotland) and the English Court of Chivalry, although there were no doubt minor differences of application. Consequently, a *prima facie* case is thus established that this English Court must have, broadly speaking, evaluated *noblesse* in much the same way as we have found it was in Scotland—where a grant of a coat of arms constituted (and still constitutes) nobilitation.

If, however, there should be any doubt left in anyone's mind as

---

[1] *Reports of Heraldic Cases in the Court of Chivalry*, 1623-1732, by G. B. Squibb, Q.C., Harleian Society, Vol. CVII, London, 1956, p. v.

to the truth of this statement, it is surely set at rest by an examination of the kinds of cases which were heard before the Earl Marshal's Court, which Mr. Squibb has summarised in his work on this subject.

The cases coming before this court are of several kinds. One that was very common was the type which was concerned with scurrilous and slanderous words about a person. This could lead to the demanding of a duel to settle the issue, where the parties were noble. As a consequence, according to a statute of the reign of Richard II of England, such actions were brought under the control of the Earl Marshal's Court.

These cases were such as the following—

Mantell v. Samson, 1635. In this " the libel alleged that the Defendant said that the Plaintiff *was no gentleman,* and that his father's coat was so old that it was threadbare ". In connection with which one of the witnesses called for the plaintiff affirmed that he had been to " the house of Walter Mantell, esq., Plaintiff's father, and *seen his coat of arms* ".[1] The upshot of which was that in 1637 judgment was given against the defendant.[2]

Leeming v. Clopton, 1637. " This was a cause of scandalous words provocative of a duel, promoted by John Leeming against William Clopton for saying that the Plaintiff *'was a base knave, a base fellowe, and could shew no Armes '*." [3]

Spencer v. Jackson, 1640. " This was a cause of scandalous words provocative of a duel, promoted by Edward Spencer of St. Neots, co. Huntingdon, gent., against John Jackson of the same . . . The following witnesses gave evidence on behalf of the Plaintiff at the Cross Keys Inn in St. Neots—

1. Robert Johnson of St. Neots, sadler ; born there ; aged 63. The parties quarrelled and Defendant said to Plaintiff " *You are noe gentleman,* because you bound yor selfe an Apprentice. *Yor binding of yor selfe apprentice doth take off yor gentility, untill such tyme as you sue out yor Coate of Armes,* which any man may doe for forty shillings." . . .

---

[1] The italics here and in the following extracts are ours.
[2] *Reports of Heraldic Cases in the Court of Chivalry, op. cit.,* pp. 21-22.
[3] *Ut supra,* p. 25.

E

    4. Robert Payne of Wintringham in St. Neots, esq., J.P. for
        Huntingdonshire ; born there ; aged 66.

Deponent knew Plaintiff's father, Robert Spencer, of Cople, co.
Bedford, who was accounted an esquire of an ancient family of gentry.
Nicholas Spencer, the eldest son of Robert, was an esquire and J.P. for
Bedfordshire, and his son Nicholas is now an esquire living at Cople.
Plaintiff lived in Cambridge with Mr. Craddocke, but whether as an
apprentice or not Deponent does not know . . .

    6. John Kempe of St. Neots, barber ; born there ; aged 68.

Plaintiff replied to Defendant " *Can you be a gentleman for forty shillings
when Raphe Bromsale (who is a man of great estate) could not be a gentleman ?* " [1]

    Besides such cases there are others which are taken by the heraldic
officers or promoted by other persons themselves against parties for
infringing the Laws of Arms.   Among such are—

> *Stepkin v Dobbin* [2], 1638, which was " promoted by John Stepkin of Stepney,
> co. Middlesex, gent., against Daniel Dobbins of the City of London,
> for writing himself ' *Esquire* ' *and assuming a coat of arms* ".   In this case we
> read that on the 9th May 1638 " The Earl Marshal ordered the Kings of
> Arms to certify their opinion of the evidences, instruments and exhibits, and
> also of an escutcheon of arms exhibited on the part of the Defendant, and
> whether the arms belonged to the Defendant by hereditary right, and by what
> right the Defendant assumed the name of ' Esquire '."

In answer to this we learn that on the 1st June 1638—

> Garter, Clarenceux and Norroy Kings of Arms certified that they did
> not find by anything produced before them that the Defendant was, or any
> of his ancestors had been, *gentlemen of coat armour*, but found that his grandfather
> and some other of his name inhabiting about that place where his father
> then dwelt were written gentlemen in divers evidences.   They did not find
> the escutcheon of arms produced in Court to belong to the Defendant or his
> ancestors, nor that the Defendant had any right to call himself " Esquire ".
>
> *By the definitive sentence it was declared that the Defendant and his ancestors were
> plebeians and not gentlemen, and had no right to assume or bear arms*, and that the
> Defendant had assumed arms and titles of " gentleman " and " esquire ".
> The Defendant was ordered to make submission, to enter into a bond for his
> good behaviour, to pay a fine of £20 and £20 costs.
>
>   The Defendant petitioned the Earl Marshal, alleging that the Plaintiff,
> " whose malice hath not end or lymitt," required him to perform the sentence
> in the most ignominious and disgraceful manner at the open sessions at

[1] *Ut supra*, p. 46.

Worcester, and to confess himself and his ancestors to be plebeians and not gentlemen. The Defendant further alleged that the heralds had never denied that he and his ancestors were gentlemen, and prayed for the execution of the sentence to be suspended until he made it appear to the Earl Marshal that he was a gentleman of ancient descent, and that the deeds and writings which he had produced to prove his descent and birth might be returned to him.[1]

(The Earl Marshal assented to this petition, but what was the outcome is not given.)

Reading over these cases, and many more which it would be tedious to cite, it is evident that so far as the Court of Chivalry of England was concerned there was a clear association between the lawful bearing of arms and the ranks of noblesse, whether gentle or esquiral—the significance of which we will discuss at some length in a later chapter.

In some of the cases the association is as plain as words can make them, as in that of Wyke v. Ems, where the Plaintiff, in 1688 " In order *to prove his gentility . . . put in evidence the following certificate, pedigree and affidavit*—July 19th 1688. These are to Certifie whom it may concerne, That *the Armes hereunder painted (viz.)* . . . belonged to the Family of Wykes of the City of Westminster in ye County of Midd ". Following this was given the pedigree.[2] If gentry had nothing to do with arms why do these defendants put in arms ?

In the case of Lloyd, Queen's Advocate of the Court, against Sir James Collett in 1707 we read that the defendant " *unlawfully had used arms* " to which he was not entitled painted on his coach " *to the prejudice of the nobility and gentry of the kingdom of England.*"[3] If arms are not proof of nobility or gentry what concern was it of these orders of society what Sir James Collett had painted on his coach in 1697 ?

In the case which Sir Richard St. George, Clarenceux King of Arms took against Thomas Tuckfield, of Fulford and Crediton, Co. Devon, in 1637, we read that the Defendant's father had been proclaimed no gentleman at the Visitation of Devon in 1620 " yet he caused a monument to his father to be erected in Crediton church and placed thereon as the arms of his family a shield—" *Argent, three fucells sable* "—and attached the appellation of " esquire " to his father's name. The Promovents claimed that the Defendant might

---

[1] *Ut supra*, pp. 30 and 32.   [2] *Ut supra*, p. 70.   [3] *Ut supra*, p. 107.

be publicly declared and *proclaimed to be no gentleman, enjoined not to bear the said arms or any arms*, and condemned in costs according to the laws and customs of arms."[1]   (Judgment was entered for the Promovents—Sir Richard St. George, and Sir Henry St. George, Richmond Herald, his surrogate).

If gentility were not resident in arms why should the promovents demand, and the Court concur, not merely in the denial to Thomas Tuckfield of the description of either gentleman or esquire, but at the same time demand that he be ordered to forbear from using not only arms to which he had no proven right, but that he be forbidden to use any arms at all ?

It seems inconceivable to us that, in English heraldic law, not only as we have outlined it from its great authorities in the previous chapter, but also from the actual recorded cases in the Earl Marshal's Court, it can ever be argued again that the Law of Arms in England is not the bedrock upon which nobility, in the broad international use of that term in which we use it in this book, is founded.

Mr. G. D. Squibb, in his latest book,[2] dealing with the cases in the Earl Marshal's Court of England, infers in connection with some of the cases that gentility was not at this time dependent on the possession of armorial bearings. That is certainly true enough if we say that it was not *entirely* dependent on the possession of arms. Since nobility had existed before arms, and it was conceivable that some noble families could have survived who had never borne arms, and since, in any case, in some realms (such as Greece and Armenia) heraldry did not exist, and since also it was equally conceivable that in some occasional families the occupation of noble offices could have occurred over several generations, whereby a presumptive claim might be made to gentility, no one is going to say absolutely and definitively that it is absolutely impossible to be noble without arms. Consequently, a litigant in the Court having no arms on which to rely, had to fall back on making out a case, if he could, based upon other principles of assessing nobility, such as those we have just mentioned and hope if it were possible to succeed on those grounds. But the fact remains

---

[1] *Ut supra*, p. 24.

[2] *The High Court of Chivalry*, Clarendon Press, Oxford, 1959.

that the assize or sasine of arms was the clear and absolute evidence of nobility, acceptable outside the Court by all society, and within it absolutely as proof beyond which it was not strictly necessary to go.

Nobility may, conceivably, be demonstrable by some non-armigers, but they have to prove their nobility on each and every occasion it is challenged, and in the end have to have recourse to the expensive and hazardous process of litigation before the Court of Chivalry. The cases which Mr. Squibb has so ably quoted in his various works on this subject illustrate to what twists and turns such litigants were put, in the hope of establishing that which would have been demonstrable at once had they possessed the *tesserae nobilitatis*—the warranty of nobility, which is established by proved inheritance or possession of the relevant armorial bearings. Arms are the title deeds of nobility, and a non-armiger who claimed to be noble before the Court was like a man who had no title deeds to show his right to the land which he claimed. It might be his, but he had to prove it, and prove it most convincingly, and with a superabundance of all relevant evidence which could be adduced—and this was no easy or inexpensive thing to do.

Something should also be said, *en passant*, concerning the " buying " of a coat of arms, of which we have seen something in the provocative words hurled at certain individuals in the foregoing cases by those who were abusing them. From the deposition of one of the witnesses is given the answer to the argument that anybody could buy arms, and with it his nobility. It is overlooked that arms can only be bestowed on worthy and virtuous persons who come within certain categories, which are those which are reckoned as having achieved in themselves personal nobility—such as the list set out earlier by Rose-haugh, and supported by similar categories listed by the English heralds of the same period.

As a consequence, Raphe Bromsale, whom the witness names, although a rich man, could not receive arms, because he had not yet reached a personal state of nobility in his way of life and bearing. Thus the forty shillings fee for a grant of arms at that time, was not a buying of arms in the strict sense of that term, as much as the paying of the fees for the patent which recognised the petitioner as a noble, and which gave him in it the *tesserae nobilitatis*, in his coat of arms.

CHAPTER VI

THE CONTINUED SIGNIFICANCE OF ARMS IN THE BRITISH REALMS FROM THE 17th-18th CENTURIES TO THE PRESENT TIME

THE evidence which we have covered leaves no doubt that arms, however they were acquired, by original nobility of race, with or without prescriptive assumption of arms, or by ennoblement and grant at a subsequent date, were, so far as Scotland and England are concerned, the only self-evident criteria of nobility till the times with which we have dealt, and which were the end of the seventeenth century to the first half of the eighteenth. We have not discussed directly Irish heraldry, because the material on which to draw is not quite so extensive as that of England. But since Irish heraldry in almost all its characteristics was parallel to English, it can be assumed that what has been said in connection with the latter applies with equal force to the former.

In the period that has lapsed since these times there has been no change in the law of Scotland which would invalidate in any way the Acts of the Scottish Parliament of 1592 and 1672, and other statutes under which Scottish heraldry has been administered. On the contrary, instead of any derogation from the authority of the supreme court of chivalry in Scotland, the Lyon Court, and that of the Lord Lyon King of Arms, and his officers at arms, a Royal Commission of 1822 made recommendations which in certain respects were designed to make the older acts more efficient in modern circumstances, and these were incorporated into the Statutes of 30 and 31, Victoria, Cap. 17, since when, as the present Lord Lyon, Innes of Learney, says in his most important exposition of *Scots Heraldry*,[1] " there has been no difficulty in enforcing the law with the same wholesome vigour shown in the seventeenth and eighteenth centuries ".

We may add to that the additional statement from Sir Thomas Innes of Learney,[2] that " not only has Lyon Court prosecution been sustained in the Supreme Court of Scotland so recently as 1926, but there are many buildings in Scotland where arms surreptitiously erected have, on official discovery, been removed or amended at the Lord Lyon's command, perhaps the most spectacular instances being when, in 1862, a number of heraldic stained-glass windows were removed from Glasgow Cathedral, and when in 1927 the Government approved in Parliament the orders of the Lord Lyon, by which a number of bogus County and Burgh arms were razed off the walls of the Scottish National War Memorial ".

Therefore the Law of Arms as administered in Scotland stands exactly where it did in 1672, and what a coat of arms implied then it still does to this day. There is no question of there having been any evolution of a new concept of the meaning of arms, for the statutes under which the Lyon Court functions are explicit, as any reference to the Act of 1672 printed in the Appendix to *Scots Heraldry* will make quite clear.

However, if there should be any lingering doubts in anyone's mind that this can be, in view of strenuous attempts made in some quarters in England and America to try to show that arms today have no nobiliary significance, a glance at a Scottish grant of arms will make it quite apparent that heraldry means in Scotland in 1961 exactly what it meant four centuries earlier. For in such a grant the Lyon Court is very rightly, and properly, explicit in the concession which it is making on behalf of the Crown of Scotland. We would venture to say that to fail to be categoric in an important legal document of this kind, and to leave it ambiguous, subject to varying interpretations, would be a serious failure of the Lord Lyon to exercise his offices correctly. Especially is this the case at such a time as this when it is known that certain persons have indulged in a serious

[1] *Scots Heraldry*, 1956, pp. 80-81.
[2] *Ut supra*, pp. 81-82.

controversial advocacy elsewhere to try to imply (for they cannot prove their assertions) that arms are not *tesserae nobilitatis*.

Thus it is that in every Scottish grant of arms today will be read, after the description of the armorial bearings—" by demonstration of which Ensigns Armorial, *Insignia of Nobility, he and his successors in the same are, amongst all Nobles and in all Places of Honour, to be taken, numbered, accounted and received as Nobles in the Noblesse of Scotland* ". It will be noted that this is substantially the same formula as is found in the grant by Clarenceux King of Arms in 1494 which we have cited earlier.

No one who has studied Scottish heraldic practice, as part of the legal system of Scotland, can possibly do other than accept the facts as we have interpreted them. It is worth noting that Mr. L. G. Pine,[1] a contemporary English writer, in his recent work, while highly critical in places of the administration of English heraldry, does not attempt to be so where Scottish is concerned. On the contrary he acknowledges that Scottish heraldry began as in other feudal lands, is backed by the Statutes of 1672 of the Scottish Parliament and of 1867 of the Union Parliament, and rests upon 300 years of continuous practice and law, of a highly scientific nature.

It is incontrovertible that a Scottish grant of arms now, as in the past, confers a confirmation of, and legal admission into, the Noblesse of Scotland.

We have dealt briefly with Scotland first, in considering the modern practice and valuation of heraldry, because the facts are so apparent that there can be no controversy as to the nature, implication and meaning of a legally acknowledged coat of arms in Scotland.

We have seen that English and Scottish heraldic practices were fundamentally identical, and meant an acceptance of the nobiliary status of arms throughout Stuart times. The fact that in Scotland we have established that that status continues with all the force of law behind it, would suggest that whatever ambiguities there may be in later English practice and legal pronouncements, in general, arms must mean one thing only to the common Crown. It cannot seriously be argued that in its capacity as that of Scotland arms are one thing

---

[1] *Heraldry & Genealogy.* The English Universities Press, 1957, pp. 110-111.

and quite another in that of England. Therefore, the presumption is that English arms must continue to be ensigns of nobility. Without arms no one has clearly demonstrable hereditary nobility, unless he is a peer without arms—as sometimes occurs today. Furthermore, this is a view which has been re-iterated on high English authority in this century. Thus, in Halsbury's *Laws of England*[1] W. A. Lindsay, K.C., Norroy King of Arms stated—" It is still the law that no man is entitled to the *dignity* of a Gentleman and to the armorial insignia except by record, and that such record exists only in the College of Arms." Furthermore, in the case of *Manchester Corporation* v. *Manchester Palace of Varieties* tried in 1954 with Lord Chief Justice Goddard as Surrogate it was accepted that a coat of arms was a *dignity*, which must mean a nobiliary rank.[2] Lord Crawford's statement is, therefore, amply justified when he says—" Every British gentleman entitled to bear coat-armour is noble whether titled or not. It is only in comparatively recent times that this has been forgotten ".[3]

The argument, therefore, that a grant from the British Crown, as the Scottish Crown, being set out *in forma meliori* consists of Letters of Ennoblement, whereas a grant from the same Crown, *qua* that of England, being set out *in forma communi*, does not, seems to have little weight. It is, perhaps, a pity that gradually English patents have changed their form from the type we have seen employed by Clarenceux in 1494, which like a Scottish grant today is unquestionably an ennoblement and specifically says so. But, even if the English grant does not say so, it says that the arms are granted according to the *Law of Arms*, and until it can be shown that the law has been changed in England it must be presumed that the arms conferred are noble arms as they are still in Scotland, and as they always were in both kingdoms.

An argument usually put forward was that whatever the law was in the times of the visitations it had fallen into disuetude, since the Court Martial (the Earl Marshal's Court), the supreme Court of Chivalry in

---

[1] 1912, Vol. XXII, p. 289.

[2] *A Verbatim Report of the case in The High Court of Chivalry of the Lord Mayor, Aldermen and Citizens of Manchester versus The Manchester Palace of Varieties Ltd. on Tuesday, 21st December, 1954.* Heraldry Soc., 1955, p. 54.

[3] The Earl of Crawford, *Lives of the Lindsays*, Vol. I, p. 227.

England, equivalent to the Lyon Court in Scotland, had ceased to function, and so where the nobiliary law, or the Law of Arms, ceases to be enforceable there is no law. As a consequence what may have been good law in the seventeenth century ceased to be in the twentieth century.

Since the Earl Marshal's Court ceased to sit from 1735, this argument had some apparent weight, even if it then led to the illogicality that a Scottish coat of arms was of value and an English one meant nothing at all ! Which, of course, is a preposterous situation. However, since *The Lord Mayor, Aldermen and Citizens of the City*

Earl Marshal of England

College of Arms

of Manchester brought their action in the Court of Chivalry in 1954 against *Manchester Palace of Varieties Ltd.*, for wrongful use of the City's arms this argument is no longer valid. For it has been demonstrated that the Court does exist, and it can be used. It is not, admittedly, as effective an instrument, as is the Lyon Court. But that is due to the fact that the English heralds have not the backing of the precise statutes under which Scottish heraldic practice is continued. But they have demonstrated that the relief is there for any one wronged in his rights under the Law of Arms. Consequently, it is hard to see how anyone can any longer hope to argue effectively that the Law of Arms in Scotland may mean that arms are feudal heritage of a nobiliary nature, but in England they are something quite different.

Those English and American writers who continue to stress that arms are nothing in England, but some glorified kind of hereditary

rebus, trade mark or monomark, have therefore had to have recourse
to other arguments. Among these are to turn attention to the nature
of arms outside of the realms of England, Scotland and Ireland, and
to try to establish that in other countries arms have no nobiliary
significance. This, in fact, they cannot do effectively, as we shall
seek to show later, although we readily admit that sometimes, in some
overseas realms, arms do not necessarily carry the same connotation
per se, without an additional patent of nobility. This line of argument
overlooks entirely the fact that we are concerned with the nature
of arms and their implication as under the Scottish, English, and,
formerly, Irish Crowns.

A second line of argument is that nobility cannot be purchased
whereas a coat of arms is bought since fees are paid for it. This, so
they say, proves that arms do not carry nobiliary status. This argument
is a particularly shallow one, although intended to appeal to the
prejudices of our own age, and to exploit the undoubted ignorance
of the mass of educated people in this particular field. We would
respond that while nobility ought not to be bought, and by a strict and
just interpretation of nobiliary law it cannot be, in fact even peerage
has been in living memory the subject of political party financial
transactions. In one of the more respectable Sunday newspapers
during 1958 the memoirs relating to an oil magnate were given, in
which it was said that he had been asked during or about the time of
the first world war for £100,000 in return for being made a Lord of
Parliament, and he had turned it down as too high a price to pay!
If then, peerages have, unfortunately, been subject to such sordid
transactions, and yet remain absolutely legal and effective, conferring
upon the peer and his heir nobility (irrespective of whether they have
arms or not), then the whole argument that since a coat is bought,
this invalidates the nobility of the status of arms, falls entirely to the
ground.

However, there is a further consideration which is relevant.
Nothing is bought which is the subject of a *petition*. The petitioner for
arms has no right to demand the arms, or to enforce the sale of arms.
The College of Arms may say, as it does, that its scale of fees are
£131, 5s. for a grant of English arms. This is not an offer for sale of

the arms, and the petitioner cannot in any court of English law enforce the sale of the arms to himself. Therefore the arms are not bought, they are conferred by the Crown, acting through the Earl Marshal and the Kings of Arms, in accordance with the Law of Arms, to a petitioner who has humbly prayed for them to be conceded.

The fees paid are analogous to the fees which were paid up to the first world war by all peers.[1] It was only on so many service chiefs having peerages conferred upon them, at that time, and the fact that they represented that they could not afford to pay them, that such fees were remitted. The *nobiles majores* have been relieved of these exactions, but the *nobiles minores* have not.

Furthermore, on the continent exactly the same procedure was followed in connection with ennoblement as here in connection with a grant of arms. In France a petitioner had to solicit letters of nobilitation, and in Austria for the title of Baron,[2] and in each case the appropriate fees had to be paid—but the nobilitation was not bought, since it would not have been granted if the petitioner had not obtained the status which enabled him to put forward his petition or the Crown had wished for any other reason to refuse it. However, once the letters patent of nobility or barony had been granted they had all the force and respectability of law behind them, and gave their recipients their proper places in the tables of precedence. Consequently, the procedure followed by the English, Scottish and Irish heralds is the ancient one which was common throughout most if not all of Europe in the past.

It has been alleged that today anyone can receive arms from the College of Arms for the mere fact of paying for them. Even if this were so, it would neither be an entirely unique occurrence, since we know that venial heralds in the past have misused their office—and been punished for doing so—nor would it, for all that, alter the validity of the patent of arms, nor the legal rights in nobiliary law which the grantee would have received. But, we are assured, by

---

[1] Or the chancery fees of one kind or another paid in many of the orders of knighthood—in Britain, for instance, in the Venerable Order of St. John, or, elsewhere, in such orders as Malta and Constantine St. George.

[2] Sir James Lawrence, Knight of Malta. *On the Nobility of the British Gentry*, Paris, 1828.

officers of arms at the College that Garter expects every officer to vouch for the petitioner, and, in other words, the old criterion of nobility of occupation and the arrival at the " port of a gentleman " are expected of the petitioners.

An approach to the College of Arms for a grant, as Mr. L. G. Pine quite specifically points out in his useful work on *Heraldry and Genealogy*,[1] is an approach to the Queen as the Fountain of Honour. In which case, a coat of arms is an honour. It seems quite impossible to so regard it if it does not confer that nobiliary status which has always been inherent within a grant of arms in the past. Otherwise, how can a licence to have a particular pattern on a shield be any more an honour than to obtain a trade mark? What is this honour, in terms of nobiliary law, if it is not ennoblement? We know, in the English legal system, or in the Scottish, of no other forms or categories of honours from the Fountain of Honour, excepting those which were comprehended within, and taken cognizance of, by the Law of Arms.

The distinguished eighteenth century English heraldic writer, Edmondson, particularly emphasises the fact that arms are badges of *honour*. For instance in one passage he says (the italics are ours)—

> " Heraldry . . . is to be considered, *not only as the science of armories and their blazons*, but as comprehending a perfect knowledge of whatever relates to several military *marks of honour and dignity* . . . which have been assumed by sovereigns, appropriated to communities and high office, or, *according to the laws of arms, have been either taken, and authorised to be retained, or originally granted by potentates*, or such as they have duly authorised for that purpose, as hereditary tokens, *whereby families and persons of ancient and worthy descent are not only illustrated*, distinguished, and differenced among themselves, *but separated and known from the ignoble and common ranks of people, who are not entitled to use such badges of honour and respect* [2]".

Because these ensigns are badges of honour we find that distinguished men of all fields of activity have coveted them, and we think that this explains why men like William Shakespeare, whose distinction in his own field was outstanding beyond all that of the rest of the world, was not satisfied until he had also achieved the right to arms.[3]

---

[1] *Op. cit.*, p. 124.

[2] Joseph Edmondson, *A Complete Body of Heraldry*, London, 1780, Vol. I.

[3] C. W. Scott-Giles, in *Shakespeare's Heraldry*, London, 1950, pp. 27 ff. gives a full account of all the steps taken to obtain his arms, which were granted.

As some have expressed surprise that a man of Shakespeare's status should have wished to obtain this form of distinction we would say *en passant*, that this ambition to possess *tesserae gentilitae* as Edmondson reminds us, " have been sought after . . . by the ablest statesmen and greatest generals ".[1] It is as laudable, or more so, as any other natural ambition of the able man. Some find their satisfaction in laureation by their University, others in the freedom of their city,

others in a knighthood from the Sovereign. But all these are for *personal* glory. Shakespeare sought to ennoble his *family* and lift not only himself but his household as a whole—and that seems to us to be a more laudable ambition, as it is something which is shared with others, and not for just personal aggrandizement. We might also add that Robert Burns, who in his own field is Shakespeare's peer, was equally moved by the same ambition, and he tells us that he searched the records of the Lyon Court in the vain hope of finding he was of an armigerous name. When he found he was not,

William Shakespeare

struggling as he was with bitter poverty, and probably unadvised as to what he should do, he rather pathetically made up his own " coat of arms ". Had he lived long enough to have received a sufficient meed of success in his lifetime it is more than likely that he would have petitioned for arms, and the Sovereign (acting through his Commissioner, the Lord Lyon) would have crowned his distinction with them. What ambition is good enough to be the goal of a William Shakespeare or a Robert Burns cannot be dismissed with a sneer as contemptible.

However to return to our subject.

All the evidence leads categorically to the conclusion which Mr. Hankinson, the learned editor of the current *Debrett's Peerage*,[2] gives when he defines the rank of gentleman as that " which strictly speaking is the gentility conferred by the lawful bearing of arms, and is in that sense equivalent to the word nobleman ". John Cussans, earlier, says

[1] *Op. cit.*
[2] 1957, p. 183.

the same thing. " Gentlemen are all these who, lawfully (are) entitled to Armorial distinction ".[1]

Unfortunately, in some quarters, there is an entirely subjective approach to this matter. In the emotional heat which is generated, the whole of the conclusions to be drawn of the Laws of Arms is quite disregarded. This is sometimes seen in the well-educated man of ample means, with perhaps several generations behind him in that style, who rests upon the power which wealth has given—since his ancestors in the industrial revolution (or at some other date in history) made the means which have enabled him to achieve that way of life. If his forbears had no known right to arms, and he himself has taken no steps to rectify the matter, he often tends to become indignant at not being automatically received as a *gentleman* in nobiliary law. Was he not at Eton ? Does he not rub shoulders in his club with Peers and Members of Parliament ? Has he not an ample estate in the Shires ? Is he not already calling his a " County " family ? Why then should he humble himself by presenting a petition to the Earl Marshal to be made a gentleman ?

There is no doubt that it was this opulent capitalist class, of the Forsyte Saga genre, that was grossly offended with Fox-Davies when in the first quarter of this century he began publishing his works on heraldry.[2] Although not for the first time in England since the eighteenth century attention had been drawn to the need for arms to prove gentility, Fox-Davies laid special emphasis on the legal aspects of heraldry in this connection.

No one denies that such people have arrived at " the port of a gentleman " and they are eligible to receive arms, and to be taken and received, accounted and known by the Sovereign in the ranks of the

[1] *Handbook of Heraldry*, London, 1882, p. 215.
[2] Fox-Davies was bitterly assailed, and called an ignoramus, no scholar, and similar things. As a lawyer, he had certainly legal knowledge, and that was badly needed in expositions of English heraldry at that time. We are by no means in agreement with Fox-Davies, in all he wrote, as we feel that he was too strongly influenced by English Common law in interpreting Nobiliary Law (such as, for instance, in the question of bastardy) and of some of the concepts of heraldry in both its international and Scottish ramifications he had little knowledge, but, for all that, we think that his monumental works which did so much to put heraldry on a proper footing, will survive and rise superior to his critics.

Noblesse of the kingdom.   But until they have received the Letters Patent they are only able to insist upon being called gentry as an act of courtesy and not of right.[1] Furthermore, if any of them wished to be accepted in the rank of honour and devotion, in the Sovereign Military Order of Malta or in Constantinian St. George, or other famous orders of Chivalry, where proofs of nobility are required, they would simply have to be denied, because they would not be able to

Lawrence

produce the necessary arms, as the *tesserae gentilitatis* on the basis of which their claims to be gentlemen would have to rest.[2]   The same thing is true in the case of any alliance by way of marriage which their families might wish to make with any of the older and legitimist families in Europe.   Indeed, there are certain exclusive clubs to which they could not be admitted in certain continental cities.

It is not unusual, it should be observed, to find that some of the people in this category use self-assumed or someone else's arms, or more probably crests, on their silver-ware.   Stephen Martin Leake, a former Garter King of Arms, referred to such people as " apochryphal gentlemen ".[3]

As Sir James Lawrence, K.M., in his book *On the Nobility of the British Gentry*, pointed out long ago (when he published his book in Paris in 1828) every family has to have a beginning, and there is

[1] Short of bringing the matter, by expensive and hazardous litigation, into the Court of Chivalry, and, if they can, establishing their right on the basis of continued occupancy for several generations of noble-offices, or similar criteria.   Short of possession of arms a definite pronouncement of the Court, or of the Crown in some other way, is absolutely essential.

[2] It is doubtful if the findings of a Court of Chivalry that a candidate was noble on extraneous grounds other than by the possession of armorial bearings would be considered sufficient evidence of nobility in most orders of chivalry which demand proofs of nobility for admission to noble grades.   Moreover, even the pronouncement of the Crown in Commissions, where it might designate an officer or a magistrate a gentleman or esquire would be considered insufficient, as these would be taken to refer to personal nobility arising from the holding of such noble offices.

[3] Joseph Edmondson, *op. cit.*, p. 154, quoting *Maitlands' History of London*, Vol. II, p. 836.

therefore no disgrace in those who have arrived at the " port " of gentry in facing the fact and petitioning for arms, and so becoming accepted legally as within the noblesse of the realm.

Be all that as it may, as we have traced the Laws of Arms in Scotland and England, there is not the slightest doubt that they are basically the same in either country in their nature and implication, and that those principles of law which operated in the seventeenth century still prevail today, and whether people like it or not, Arms in the British Isles are *tesserae nobilitatis*, and the main means of establishing hereditary membership of the noblesse of the land. Many others may consider themselves *socially* gentry, but they cannot demand it as of *legal* right without validly recognised arms,[1] for which they must petition the Sovereign through the Kings of Arms who are the Commissioners for Noblesse. As the present erudite Lord Lyon says of a Scottish grant of Arms (which we believe is equally applicable to an English or Irish)—" A Patent of Arms is—and I say this with full official weight—a Diploma of Nobility. . . . The effect of a Grant of Arms in Scotland is to confer . . . a formal recognition by the Crown that the grantee and all his descendants—members of his ' Family '— are noble".[2]

One recent English writer has said that if a present day English grant confers nobility it is " some sort of pseudo-nobility " and invites and deserves only ridicule and contempt ".[3] This is as may be. We have shown what nobility is *under the law*, and under that law all armigers are nobles, and their nobility will be acknowledged when advanced on the basis of *assize of arms* and genealogy by all orders of knighthood which require *proofs of nobility* from our own Venerable Order of St. John to those of the continent of Europe. Without such evidence of nobility a cadet of a *non-armigerous peer of the realm* would, not, for instance, be able to establish without any question that he was a *noble* or of *noble birth*. To advance himself without arms would only

[1] Or a favourable decision in the Court of Chivalry of ancient nobility on other grounds than those of arms alone. It might also be pointed out that it is doubtful if a non-armigerous peer could qualify for anything other than *nobility*—as we have never had any instance of an old nobility (that is gentility) in a non-armigerous peer.

[2] *Scots Heraldry*, pp. 91-95.

[3] A. E. S. Bradshaw, *The Coat of Arms*, Vol. V, No. 37, Jan. 1959, p. 166.

F

invite " ridicule and contempt ".   In any case what is founded in the international nobiliary law of western Europe, in the laws of England as well as those of Scotland, and which still provides the basis of accreditation in high circles and important orders, does not invite " contempt and ridicule ".   That rather rebounds on those who, refusing to face facts (often for quite subjective reasons), persist in a usage of terms which have no warranty in the Laws of Arms.   We are rather inclined to think that the person of simple origins who by education and social position has reached the " port of a gentleman " and persists in calling himself one, yet refuses to ask the Queen, through the Kings of Arms, to make him a gentleman of coat armour[1] is rather the pseudo-gentleman, and inviting " contempt and ridicule ", and not the person who, " obtempering the law " realises that it is incumbent upon him to be the starter of a new stock in the noblesse of the realm.

If, however, certain amateur English heraldic enthusiasts refuse to accept for an English grant of arms the evidence which we have given for the nobiliary status of English arms, then all they succeed in doing is to devalue them.   They make them of no account or value compared with those of Scotland, the nobiliary character of which are established beyond question, from the earlier acts down to the latest pronouncements of the present Lord Lyon.   They are at liberty to attempt to devalue their own country's coinage in this respect but not that of Scotland.   Furthermore, if they think that arms in Scotland constitute no nobiliary status let them come north of the Border and make a permanent public display of arms unrecognised by the Scottish Crown, or attempt, without standing on the assize or laws of arms, to be received in the ranks of esquire or gentry on any state occasion.   They will very soon be disillusioned by the application of this very nobiliary law against them.   Having been duly mulcted by the Court one can safely say where the ridicule and contempt will lie.   On the other hand, let an Englishman formally produce a valid English coat of arms as his evidence of gentry, and he will find that in Scotland it will be accepted as of sterling worth,

---

[1] And fails to take the alternative course, if he can establish his claim that he is entitled to be accepted as a noble, by litigation before the Court of Chivalry.

and such an Englishman will be accorded his due rank and precedency on an official occasion when he needs to be placed among the noblesse of Scotland.

We may also add that the action of many new made knights and peers in refusing to sue out a coat of arms is highly significant. Some have expressed surprise at such action, where we think it is entirely uncalled for, if any close consideration is given to the subject. In many cases among the knights, and in practically all among the peers, who have pursued this policy, there has been a clear understanding of the significance of a grant of arms. In a large proportion of these cases the persons concerned, like Lord Dukeston,[1] for instance, subscribe to socialist egalitarian views. They are prepared to take a peerage in order to pursue their political objectives in the House of Lords, even if it involves that which they would allege to be distasteful to themselves—their personal ennoblement. Such peers are noble in their own person, by reason of their peerage, and their heirs in succession are noble. These things they cannot escape, but their other children, who will not inherit the peerage, are not noble,[2] and can never style themselves legally as nobility or gentry. Such Socialist peers have not taken out arms because they have realised that arms (which Seton quite rightly said, are " universally regarded as the essential mark of gentility ")[3] confer hereditary nobility. Their position in this matter is quite logical, and it is evident that they are more aware of the implication of the meaning of arms than some of those who have been trying to propagate the idea that the Laws of Arms ceased to be effective after the Visitations in England.

Some reference should be made, in closing this chapter, to the curious English use of the term *ennoblement* in the Letters Patent of Peerage where we read " We . . . really ennoble him ". This has led some to argue that the only nobility in England is that of peerage,[4]

---

[1] Who according to L. G. Pine, *Heraldry & Genealogy*, London, 1957, p. 130, is not armigerous.

[2] Unless they continue to hold noble offices for successive generations, and so establish by a kind of presumptive right the claim to be received as gentry. This a Court of Chivalry might well accept.

[3] George Seton, Advocate, *The Law and Practice of Heraldry in Scotland*, 1863, p. 5.

[4] See remarks in the Editorial, *The Coat of Arms*, Vol. V, No. 37, Jan. 1959.

which is wholly inconsistent with all the other evidence we have thus far discussed. In many cases, of course, the new peer is a plebeian, having neither arms nor knighthood nor baronetcy, nor other form of personal nobility. But in other cases the new peer is already noble, and such an expression as *ennoblement* in such a context is superfluous. It can only be used through sheer ignorance of the draughtsmen of the letters patent over the last century or so. How obviously this is the case is clearly proved from the elevations to the various ranks of the peerage of the Duke of Wellington. When he was made a peer in 1809 he was *ennobled*, although already a knight and the son of a peer

Duke of Wellington   Courtney, Earl of Devon

and descended of an ancient noble house ! But when he was advanced to the rank of Earl in 1812 he was again " *really ennobled* ", and again in 1812 when he was made a Marquis ! Finally, ignoring all their previous statements the Crown lawyers made the Prince Regent (acting for his father) announce in 1814 that—" by these presents for us our heirs and successors . . . we do dignify, invest and really ennoble with such name of Duke of Wellington . . ." ! [1]

The same sort of thing happened to Lord Roberts.

What are we to infer from this ? Either that in these letters patent the word means nothing at all, or, that it means (in the case of a plebeian) nobilitation in one context, and (in the case of a noble) in another, *promotion in the nobility*. No precedent can be established from the fact that Mary I of England " ennobled " in this way Edward

[1] I am indebted for this information to the Laird of Buthlaw.

Courtenay, when he was made Earl of Devon in 1553 since both his parents had been attainted. His restoration in blood was necessary. It is quite clear that the letters patent for elevation to the peerage cannot be used to overthrow the whole weight of evidence, backed by Scottish Acts of Parliament, that nobility is noblesse, as internationally understood, and that those who have received letters patent of grants of arms, and most certainly when in *forma meliori*, as in the case of Scottish patents and older English ones, have in law and fact been ennobled.

It is quite clear that it is a misuse of terms to talk of being raised to the peerage as *ennoblement* except where the new peer is a plebeian.

From a self-interest point of view it is also injurious to the English to persist in the restricted use of the term noble for peer. For in the past it has worked very much against travelling English gentlefolk, who, when asked if they were nobles, thinking it meant peers, said they were not, and so were recorded as plebeians and treated accordingly. In some cases, when in foreign service, they humiliatingly went through the ridiculous business of being ennobled by the Crown under which they served, when, being already noble, they could have asked for something more substantial by way of recognition, such as a title of peerage. Foreigners cannot be blamed if they take the Englishman's language seriously as meaning what it says, and they cannot be expected to allow for the slip-shod use of the tongue where it should be precisely employed.

Before concluding this chapter something ought to be said on the use of the term *Commoner*. For here, again, English folk who have not titles, by calling themselves Commoners put themselves in an invidious position, especially when they use it with the intent to suggest that all are Commoners below the rank of peers, whom they mistakenly allude to as nobles. The result is that outside of England it is assumed that the term commoner means the proletariat as distinct from the noblesse.

There are two historic uses of the term *Commons*.

The first certainly means non-noble, that is non-armigerous, or below the rank of gentleman and newly created noble. Thus, in the Wars of the Roses we find occasions on which orders were given that quarter was to be given to the Commons but that all gentlemen should be

put to the sword. Again, at the ill-fated Battle of Flodden we read
that Lord Lindsay said—" For if we lose the King, we lose the whole
nobility thereof, for none, my lords, have remained but gentlemen ;
the Commons are all departed from us for lack of victual ".

From this it is clear that the term *Commons* in both these cases
was used for the yeomanry, the backbone of the infantry and archer
forces of those days. Presumably it extended downwards, as necessary,
to include the common people of the land as well.

The second use of this term certainly did not mean non-noble. But in this
use it was a more legalistic one, and survives in the title of the English
lower house of Parliament—the House of Commons. That term really
means the House of the Communities of England, that is the *communitas
terrae*. Thus in the letter to Pope Alexander in 1258 we read the letter
was sent by the *communitate Angliae*. This *communitas terrae*, or *le commun
de la terre*, was sometimes spoken of as the *tota nobilitas Angliae* (all
the English nobility). At other times it was the *universitas baronagii*
(all the baronage). That the Commons of England were the nobility,
and their representatives, as distinct from the Lords who formed the
monarch's council, is evident from the name given to the members for
the Shires, who were called Knights of the Shires, and who were elected
by the gentry of each county.

At a later stage, 1265, the burgesses of the towns, who formed the
communitates civitatum were admitted to the Commons. However,
members of the cities and towns were in a markedly different position
from those of the Shires. These were ruled by a statute of Henry VI
as having to be gentlemen born, and they were allowed to wear their
spurs in the chamber, which no citizen was permitted to do. This
difference lasted on right down to the nineteenth century.

It is quite evident that the term Commons, and the resultant term
Commoner, which springs from this publicised use of the word in the
name of the lower house of the English legislature, meant originally
the community of the nobility, but was later broadened out to comprehend the representatives of all the communities of the realm—that
is the nobility (under peerage rank) and the burgesses. In recent times
it has been extended further, by universal suffrage, to comprehend
the commons, as found in the first use of the term which we have given,
whom our more outspoken ancestors would have called the vulgar.

From this, however, it is quite clear that while the term Commoner may comprehend within its meaning the non-noble, commercial, artizan and labouring sections of society, it does not necessarily do so, as it also includes the bulk of the nobility of the kingdom which is that part below peerage rank.

We suggest that when a term requires so much definition and qualification in nobiliary law in order to assess in what sense it is used, it certainly should not be employed, without being clearly defined, in works of heraldry and genealogy, nor in matters which come within the comprehension of foreign courts, officials or bodies of any kind.

Emanating from certain continental circles, and starting with a statement by Bouly de Lesdain[1] to the effect that the Scottish heraldic authority did not reject any petitioner who was a person of honourable status, and repeated by M. Paul Adam,[2] there has come the suggestion by implication that in both England and Scotland, while it may well be that arms are still controlled by the Crown, and theoretically so far as Scotland is concerned they are feudal heritage, for all that they are so easily acquired, that in fact a situation has been created by the English and Scottish authorities that it has not been necessary in the British Isles to insist on the prescriptive right to arms. For, where anyone can have arms for the mere asking, why not petition and pay the fee and have them? Thus M. Paul Adam[3] says that in England and Scotland arms are always obtained without difficulty. Even if this were so it overlooks three facts. First, that it would not alter the legal status of arms; secondly, in any case, the fees levied are quite substantial—consequently in fact they go a long way to restrict grants to people who come within the very classes who have in former ages provided the anobli; and thirdly there is in fact a close scrutiny to see that the persons are honourable in status, or as it is put in Scotland, virtuous and well-deserving persons.

That we are right in our conclusions on this matter is shown by taking the grants of arms made by the English College of Arms at, for

[1] Bouly de Lesdain, *Heraldique du Royaume-Uni*, p. 54.

[2] *De l'Acquisition et du port des armoires, Recueil du IVe Congrès international des Sciences Généalogique et Héraldique*, Brussels, 1958, p. 103.

[3] *Ut supra*, p. 105.

instance, the Tudor period, and in the nineteenth century. For every 100,000 of the population there were in the 1550-1559 period 6 anobli : in the 1570-1579 15 : in the 1820-29 10 : and in the 1890-99 less than 4.[1]

Whatever else these figures may show it is quite evident that they prove that right down to the end of the nineteenth century there is no evidence that the English Kings of Arms were any more open-handed in this matter than their Tudor predecessors, who had no hesitation in writing in their patents that a grant was attached to gentry and ennoblement. Indeed, it would seem that, if anything, the recruitment of armigerous nobility by grantees is definitely occurring at a more restrictive rate than formerly.

Armstrong-Jones

Judging by the correspondence which has occurred in continental circles and papers in April and May 1960 concerning the marriage of Mr. Armstrong-Jones and Princess Margaret there has been a suggestion that this is a misalliance. Indeed, many British people, particularly in London, among the masses, have apparently viewed the matter in the same way, but with an approval as strong as the dis-approval from the continental quarters to which we have alluded. Their sense of being the under-privileged, combined with the roman-ticism of the " court " photographer, as it were, carrying off the Princess, on almost fairy tale lines, has appealed strongly to them, and been considerably exploited by the press from that angle.

However, all this has shown a lamentable lack of knowledge of the law on the part of both these points of view.

The fact of the matter is that Mr. Anthony Armstrong-Jones is the grandson of Sir Robert Armstrong-Jones, Knight bachelor, who was a grantee of arms—an anobli so far as his hereditary nobility was concerned and noble personally by reason of his knighthood.

---

[1] Our figures are based upon the information as to grants provided by Edward Elmhirst, *The Fashion for Heraldry*, The Coat of Arms, East Knoyle, Wilts, April 1956, pp. 47 ff. We have taken the Tudor population figure as 5 million, and the nineteenth century figures are those derived from the census returns.

On Mr. Armstrong-Jones' mother's side, his grandfather, Lt.-Col. Leonard Messel, was personally noble by his army rank, and was an anobli by right of a grant of arms. Consequently, Mr. Anthony Armstrong-Jones being the third generation in strict nobiliary practice is rankable as a noble. As a consequence of this, since in both English and Scottish law, there has never been any restrictive practice limiting the marriages of the royal houses of either realm to princes only, as in some continental countries, but, on the contrary, there has always been permitted freely marriage between the noblesse and the royal house, it follows that this marriage is not a misalliance. In this practice England and Scotland follow the older, mediaeval, nobiliary law, in contradistinction to some continental lands where later accretions to that law have enforced in such circumstances morganatic marriages. Nobiliary law, however, has always allowed the competence of any noble to fight a duel with any other noble, no matter how great a peer or prince he may be (provided that he is not his own sovereign), or to marry his daughter, as circumstances might dictate. The marriage of Mr. Anthony Armstrong-Jones and Princess Margaret conforms at all points to nobiliary law in this matter. The fact that the husband followed a calling (of photographer)—which has endeared him no doubt to the Cockney masses, and caused as adverse comment, no doubt, in other directions—is something entirely beside the point. This is the more so since, as we have shown, Sir George Mackenzie and others have made it clear that no man taints his nobility by having recourse to labour—so long as it is not dishonourable—and even then he only loses or ought to leave off his gentility while he is in fact practising such a means of livelihood. In the marriage register it will be observed that the bridegroom gave his rank also as esquire. That is a nobiliary title.

We have ended this chapter by mentioning this royal marriage as it shows how relevant is the matter of arms to modern circumstances, in such a matter as this wedding.

THE NATURE OF ARMS IN SWEDEN

AS Sweden is one of the countries of Europe where an heraldic administration has been maintained, side by side with an extremely democratic system of monarchical government, it seems desirable to discuss briefly the nature of arms in that country. For it is obvious that consideration ought to be given more to the precedents provided by countries where the Law of Arms is administered than to those from lands where that law has ceased to be administered, and everyone can be his own herald.

Since Finland was for a time under the control of Sweden, and always very much under its influence, we have also added a brief note about the standing of arms in that country.

In Sweden heraldry was, until recently, under the *Riksheraldiker* or King of Arms. Now it is under a *Statsheraldiker*. The present holder of that office is our colleague, the *consultore pro lingua scandinavica* of the College of Heralds of Rome, Mr. Gunnar Scheffer. To him we are largely indebted for the detailed information about current practice in Sweden which appears in this chapter.

The *Riksheraldiker* of Sweden made the proposals of the new coats of arms for persons who were being made barons, counts, or other nobles, and the arms so constructed were incorporated in the patents issued by the Crown. *The nobilitation and the granting of arms were thus synchronised.*

Furthermore, in Sweden, as in the three realms of the British Isles, arms of burghers or citizens, such as Wappenbürger or arms of Citizenry of distinct civility, as found in the Empire, or Italy, were unknown and are still unknown to the Crown. In Sweden coats of arms have only been granted in connection with nobilitation. Owing to strong

German influence upon Swedish commerce in ancient as in modern times, it is obvious that burgher arms were bound to penetrate into the trading communities of the realm. But, owing to the fact that such arms were not recognised, and as arms could only be granted by the Crown in cases of nobilitation, these shields which burghers might have desired to adopt and perpetuate never were allowed to take root. The most common use of such non-nobiliary " arms " has been where a person needed a device for a seal in connection with his business and adopted it in the form of a coat of arms. But we are assured that such uses of " arms " were never consistently transmitted to descendants. Consequently, there is no question that arms as understood and recognised by law were only those which were permitted to nobles or conferred on nobilitation.

It is instructive to study the form which a typical patent of nobility and arms takes, as bearing out the above observations. The following extract is from the grant of letters patent to the family of Hallenborg, 6th May, 1720—

> We Fredrik . . . hereby make known that . . . Our faithful servant and judge over the hundreds of Oxie, Skytt and Vemmenhög in the province of Scania, Our beloved Svante Hallenberg, who has obtained general praise for himself as a just judge of irreproachable and honourable demeanour . . . That we herewith and in virtue of these Our Letters Patent . . . bestow and give him . . . his wife and legitimate descendants . . . nobility and the following coat of arms, namely :—

Since the institution of the House of the Nobles which occurred in 1625 the patents of nobility invariably showed the coat of arms, with one remarkable exception, which, however, proves the rule. This exception was in the case of the famous Central Asian explorer Sven Hedin in 1902. In the Patent of Nobility issued to him there was the statement that in addition to the admission to the nobility there was also the authority to " have and use that coat of arms which we on his proposal will graciously confirm separately ". A drawing of a coat of arms for Sven Hedin was actually approved by the King the following year.

The form which thus appears to have been consistent since the early seventeenth century in Sweden was based on that which had prevailed in the middle ages in its general principles.

Finally, it should be observed, that there is no evidence at any time of arms having been granted to non-nobles in Sweden, except in the case of knights of the Order of the Seraphim. But, since their knighthood made them of noble rank, although not hereditary nobles, the granting of coats of arms in such cases was no exception but a confirmation of the rule.

Not only does the foregoing make it clear that the nature of arms as understood in Sweden is identical with what we have seen to be the

Sven Hedin

case elsewhere, and particularly in Scotland, but it is confirmed by the situation which has arisen since 1902. For in that year Sven Hedin was the last person to be ennobled in Sweden. As a consequence of this, since no one has been raised to the rank of noble, it equally follows that no one could receive a grant of arms, unless he were a knight of the Order of the Seraphim. This is the position to this day.

The result is that the *Statsheraldiker's* present day functions, apart from dealing with arms and pedigrees of the existing *noblesse*, is to grant arms only to new Knights of the Seraphim, if they are not nobles by birth, and to allow arms to new corporations noble, such as public communities, towns, counties and the rest.

In connection with these latter the procedure is that the heraldic officers elaborate the blazon and provide the drawings of the proposed arms, and, in important cases, these are submitted to the government for approval, and in due course letters patent signed by the king and countersigned by a cabinet minister are issued. Military ensigns are also granted by the government. In the case of the arms for Knights of the Order of the Seraphim they are granted by the king as Lord and Master of the Orders of Knighthood.

Incidentally, an entirely new grant of arms for a Knight of the Order of the Seraphim costs, according to the scale of fees of 20th March 1959, 800 Swedish Crowns—about £55. Grants to a community are from 800 to 1200 Swedish crowns, that is from £55 to £82. These fees are comparable with those levied by the Scottish and

Irish heralds, and somewhat less than those of the College of Arms. The fact that Knights of the Order of the Seraphim have to pay these fees for arms once more emphasises the fact that on receiving armorial honours (which as we have seen in Sweden are clearly linked with elevation to the noblesse) fees have to be paid just as they had formerly in the case, in Britain, on elevation to the peerage. Consequently, the argument put forward so frequently in certain English heraldic circles that the fees paid would be tantamount to buying nobility indicates a clear misconception.

Unlike western estimations of gentility where as we have seen there is a clear tendency to distinguish, with technical terms, between the ennobled, the noble and the ancient noble (or gentleman), these distinctions are unknown in Sweden. The present *Statsheraldiker*, Mr. Gunnar Scheffer, suggests that the need for such distinctions never arose because of the firmly organised character of the Swedish House of Nobles, which was able, without difficulty, to estimate the status of any family in the realm.

Proofs of nobility have never been demanded in the case of Swedish orders of knighthood, perhaps because, in the past, they were usually conferred only on those who could prove a nobiliary position equivalent to those in other orders who proved their noble descents. On the other hand the Swedish orders are of a rather late date, 1748 and 1772, and this may well account for the absence of the demand for established proofs. In the case of the Order of St. John in Sweden, while the proofs are not demanded, owing to the character of the international Order of St. John, regard is paid to the nobility of those admitted to some extent. But formal proofs such as by four quarters or ancient lineal descent have not been demanded.

Although, in these respects there is a tendency to differentiation from some of the practices elsewhere in estimating the degree of nobility, it is quite clear that there is no hereditary nobility without arms in Sweden, and no arms known to the State without nobility (or knighthood, which, for this purpose is the same thing).

Baron Eric von Born, a Swedish Finn, and student in the heraldic field, has assured us that much the same position as that which we have outlined for Swedish heraldry is true of Finland, where, as no nobilitations have been granted since Czarist times, no arms have been officially permitted to private persons—and new arms are only allowed to public bodies.

On the other hand there is a school of thought which has attempted to argue that arms can be taken prescriptively in Sweden and that arms are not necessarily indications of nobility in that country.[1]

The Swedish heraldic authorities have always been aware that, starting first with German merchants, incomers did bring with them arms, and used them on their seals. But such uses were not recognised by the State, and, furthermore could have no protection in law. Consequently, such private armorial devices are not what we understand by arms, which are the subject of letters patent from the Crown of any state, or where they arose at a very ancient time, are capable of matriculation in the registers of the State, and their rights are upheld in the appropriate court of law.

Mr. Bo Tennberg (a Swedish-Finn) to whom we are indebted for a lengthy correspondence on this subject informs us that in the past many who were not nobles often assumed arms for their seals. As legal arms could only be obtained with a grant of nobility there was no other way in either Sweden or Finland to create arms independently of nobilitation by the Crown.

On 10th August 1762 the King of Sweden issued an edict prohibiting common men to use " noble arms and open helmet," and this law is, we believe, if we understand Mr. Bo Tennberg correctly, still in force in both Sweden and Finland. From this, as he observes, it has been taken that in this the King was only prohibiting the use of noble arms, and not arms as such.[2]

However, we are always brought back to the fact that the State, in Sweden, where there is still an heraldic authority, simply does not take cognizance of non-noble arms, but only those which have been conferred by the Crown, and these have invariably been granted with letters of nobilitation. Consequently, such assumed coats of arms are

---

[1] Paul Adam, *De L'Acquisition et du Port des Armoires, Recueil du IVe Congrès International des sciences Généalogique et Héraldique*, Brussels, 1958, pp. 98-99 ; and A. Berghman, *Borgerliga Häktvapen (Meddelanded fran Riksheraldikerämbetet)*, 1934.

[2] Such burgher arms are said to be legitimate if they are ensigned only with a closed helmet.

quite unprotected in law, and therefore in a legal sense do not exist at all.

It has been pointed out by Mr. Arvid Berghman [1] that for a very brief period the Swedish heralds did in fact place on record some of these non-noble arms.[1] But it is significant that the practice was stopped. Apparently, it was realised that such arms were not arms as recognised by the state, and so outwith of the province of the King of Arms. It is rather as though some of the armorial types of Merchants' Marks and some Rebuses of a similar shield form had found their way on to the registers of the College of Arms, and then, when the authorities realised that they were not genuine arms of noble families based on the prescriptive right of long user, they had forbidden the acceptance of any more. We would argue that the discontinuance of the recording of such " arms " was clear evidence that they were considered to be of an entirely different species from those normally placed on record in those registers.

It should also be observed that during the nineteenth century these non-noble coats disappeared from use, and it is only with the revival of interest in heraldry in the present century that there has come about this strenuous advocacy, and effort, to establish the validity of self-assumed arms at the present time. But so far as Sweden is concerned, where there is an active legal heraldic department of state, it seems that any such arguments are quite *ultra vires*. One would also have thought that even in Finland, where there is no heraldic authority, but where the corpus of Swedish law on this subject still governs the problem, that much the same position must exist—if the matter ever came to be tested legally.

It should be noted that owing to the lack of any heraldic authority in the Finnish Republic the natural desire of persons who have established for themselves a position in that society to consolidate it with a symbol of their status (which is in fact some sort of *de facto* nobility) does not exist. The consequence of this (in the absence of any authority to forbid an illegal usurpation of arms) has led in recent years to a widespread assumption of shields of arms. In fact we have here very much the same problem as exists in the United States, with

[1] Borgerliga Häktvapen, *op. cit.*

this difference that in Finland there is a basic corpus of heraldic law (even if it is not exercised) whereas none at all exists in America. The Finnish Heraldry Society at the present time, as the American counterpart, is encouraging the recording of these self-assumed arms where they are of a high standard.

However, all this, although a real dilemma for Finnish, as well as American, citizens who aspire to the use of armorial ensigns of honour, does not affect the situation as to what is the nature of arms as understood in the official Swedish and Swedo-Finnish armorial practice—and that is that arms are only recognised which are those belonging to noblemen.[1]

[1] We fully endorse the view of Dr. Jacques Descheemaeker (*Le Droit des Armoires, La Vie Judiciaire*, 7-12 March 1960, p. 5) that armorial ensigns have a considerable moral and spiritual value for the family—for all families. But we do not think that this justifies an assumption of arms. In Scotland this problem has been solved by giving practically every man and woman of the realm the right to wear the plant badge of their Clan and the Strap and Buckle badge of their Chief—so that from brooches of these symbols, to decoration motifs in their houses, all who can attach themselves to a clan have the legitimate use of heraldic charges, and as a consequence the feeling of belonging to an honourable company, whose traditions they transmit, without the need to pirate the arms of the noblesse of the realm.

We suggest that the solution in America, France, or Finland, or other lands where there is a strong desire in certain quarters to have the use of armorial ensigns by those whose legal right would not have been recognised by the Law of Arms, and the Fountain of Honour which administered it, is for some such use of the heraldic badge to be developed.

CHAPTER VIII

ARMS OF LOCAL NOBILITY

IN the evolution of kingdoms such as Scotland and England the great Earldoms were former kingdoms, or tantamount to such.[1] The Earldom of Northumberland, for instance, is a clear instance of that kind, and other earldoms such as Chester, or the Bishopric of Durham, were Palatinates, and had their own semi-autonomous status for a long time. Durham had its own parliament. In Scotland we have the Seven Earls referred to in earlier historical literature as the great magnates on whom the responsibility for the succession devolved in the event of there being no direct heir to the throne.[2]

These great Earls held courts which were hardly less splendid than those of their monarchs. The Earls of Oxford had one thousand retainers sitting down to meat with them every day. It follows that from an early stage of feudal history they had their own nobles and own officers dependent on them, and, in some cases, such as in that of the Earls of Chester, there was a decided tendency for them to confer a part of their arms on their dependers. However, despite this, the structure of the unified realm, whether of England or Scotland, was such that no distinctly localised nobility survived, and all nobles, *qua* nobles, ranked in the end equally in each realm.

The story is, however, quite different when we come to certain other realms on the continent of Europe. In Spain, for instance, a species of local noblesse arose within such provinces as those ruled by our earls. Such local nobles had a quite clearly defined status within their own province, but they were not accepted outside of that province as nobles and neither were their arms. Since they were not recorded in the rolls of the Sovereign's King of Arms it might be

[1] Frank Adam, revised by Sir Thomas Innes of Learney, *The Clans, Septs, and Regiments of the Scottish Highlands*. W. & A. K. Johnstone, Edinburgh, Vth Edition, 1955, p. 49.

[2] *Ut supra*, pp. 27, 29 and 30.

argued that here we have further evidence of the non-nobiliary use of arms. This, however, we do not think can be maintained, since such a development as this where a certain type of freeholder, holding by military tenure, is thus discriminated against is largely fortuitous.

It is instructive to follow the procedure for approving nobility in this connection in Spain. First of all the assemblies of local noblesse in the various provinces were asked to recognise a petitioner for noblesse. Then, at a later stage in the development of such noblesse into nobles of the realm we find a local noble petitioning for the confirmation of the Royal King of Arms, which was followed in due course by an exemplification of the local noble as a Castilian noble. That is he became a noble of the Royal Court of Spain.

We have, in Hungary, a similar situation. Hungary was conquered by tribes the members of which became the founders of its nobility. However, some of the greater magnates who arose in this nobiliary structure, and many of the bishops, were sufficiently powerful to maintain their own military vassals. These latter were called *praedalistae*. The *praedalistae* were not recognised as nobles within the nation as a whole, but each held land from his great overlord (*praedium*) as would a noble, and enjoyed a limited right of nobility. As time passed only the greater ecclesiastics (the Archbishop of Esztergom, the Archabbot of Pannonhalma, and the bishops of Györ and Zágráb) retained the right to *praedalistae*, and these latter, as a consequence, became known as ecclesiastical nobles.

In other countries we get instances of barons and nobles of the Church. This is particularly so in France, where we have instances of the baronies held of the Bishops of Paris. But we have no indication that they were ranked as fundamentally any lower than other nobles and, certainly, there is no question of their nobility being any less, *qua* nobility, than that of anyone else.

As we see it, local nobility is usually a stage in the evolution of the full concept of a universal nobiliary caste in which, in certain particular circumstances, owing to the pressure of the established noblesse who are in the majority in a given region, there is an attempt to prevent some particularly localised nobility rising to the same status and consequence in society as themselves. Since such local nobles had arms just as much as the noblesse of the realm, those arms must be considered as in some measure insignia of at least a restricted degree of nobility. Since, by petition to the Crown the local nobility tended to decrease in strength as its members became accepted by nobilitation into the full order of nobility of the kingdom, it may be looked upon as a purely transitory stage of *inferior* nobility.

Even here, therefore, their arms cannot be considered as without some measure of nobiliary value, although it is freely acknowledged that they were not internationally acceptable for full ranking of noblesse throughout the community of European nobles. In the tournament, or for purposes of marriage, or duel, the established nobility everywhere would have the right to refuse to treat with them as equals. When, however, such arms are recorded, or matriculated in the registers of their own or any other prince, they automatically must cease to be regarded as those of localised nobility, and they come within the rank of full nobility.

CHAPTER IX

TRIBAL ARMS IN RELATION TO HUNGARY, POLAND, SCOTLAND, WALES AND IRELAND

ON the whole we have been concerned with western European heraldry which is highly feudalised, and arose in a feudal environment. There are, however, regions of Europe which have their own heraldic jurisdiction, uses and traditions, where feudalism came late, and was imposed on a tribal foundation. Examples of these regions are, in the east, Hungary and Poland, and, in the west, the Highlands and Isles of Scotland, and Ireland and Wales.

If we take the case of Hungary, as an example of one type of tribal heraldry, we may briefly summarise the position as follows. About 896 the conquest of Hungary was completed by the 108 Magyar tribes—these were the only free people who had political rights. Such were called *nemes*, meaning, in Hungarian, noble, that is a member of a tribe. At the outset the ownership of land was based upon the conquest of tribal lands—these were *possessio primae occupationis*, lands of first occupation. They were in fact allodial lands, held under God by right of occupation. Such tribal lands were divided equally among the members of the tribe in common, and occupied according to tribal relationships. Each tribe had its own territory, *descensus*, held in common for the tribe, and divided among its families, and ultimately divided right down to individuals. Of this tribal land the part which was held by any one person was the house and its immediate environs (*mansio* and *sessio*), while the arable land, vineyards and woods, fishponds and the rest were held in common.

During the middle ages feudalism began to be imposed on this allodial structure, and certain individuals gained feudal control over a part or the whole of adjacent common lands and so the concept of the

86

manor (*praedium*) was developed, but the inhabitants of it in the village (*villa*) still held their own lands in common except for their own dwelling.

The stage at which feudalisation occurred was after A.D. 1001 when the lands of the realm not actually occupied by individuals or complete tribes became vested in the King. Out of this the Crown was able to make a grant (*donatio*) when it wished, and so this hastened the ultimate feudalisation of the society by having individuals depending from the Prince in a normal and recognisable feudal relationship.

Under the *jus regium* which thus arose the grantee had to be installed (*statutio, introductio*) in his fief, in the presence of his neighbours and the officer of the Crown (*homo regius*) within one year of the grant being made. If there was no objection within 15 days (*dies fatales*) the installation was formally conveyed to the King who then made out the letters patent.

This was for a long time the only way to obtain nobility, and in this respect we have the common feudal pattern that a fief was noble, and the holding of a noble fief conveyed with it nobility, although, often enough in some countries no one could occupy a noble fief who was not previously noble, or if he did it did not confer its nobility upon him.[1]

Obviously, in Hungary as elsewhere a time arrived when the ennoblement of individuals could not depend on the distribution of fiefs since all the lands had been occupied. This led to the evolution of the concept that patents of nobility could be issued without the grants of land. Such new nobles were called " nobles of letters patent ",

[1] Arnone, for instance, draws attention to the fact that the title associated with the land can only be taken when the new lord is himself noble, and the purchase of lands by ignoble persons does not confer the title, *inoltre un uomo rustico se avesse comprato uno feudo nobile non diventava nobile* (a countryman—yeoman—although he has bought a noble feu does not become noble), adding, that it is a commonly accepted view of the Civil Law *generositas et virtus pecuniis comparavi non possunt* (gentility and virtue cannot be bought with money). *Diritto Nobiliare Italiano, Storia ed Ordinamento*, Milan 1935, p. 16. John Bossewell, writing in 1572, quotes with approval the words of Chaucer—" Here may ye see well how that gentree is not annexed to a possession ", and adds, in the margin, " Here gentrie not annexed to possession ". *Workes of Armorie*, Fol 15. Mackenzie of Rosehaugh reinforces this point by saying—" An Heritor of Land doth not Nobilitate in all cases, even though the Heritage be very considerable ; for else a Rich man might Ennoble himself ". *The Science of Heraldry*, 1680, Edinburgh, p. 13.

significantly called *armalistae*. In other words, as the learned Lord Lyon has pointed out in Scotland, the arms themselves became the fief, and so, in Scotland, remain,[1] where they are *incorporal fiefs annoblissants*.

Thus in Hungary we get the evolution from an original tribal foundation of a feudal nobility. As elsewhere this nobility was of one order. Before, in fact, 1608 there was no difference among the nobles in rank at all, all being *una eademque nobilitas* (one and the same nobility). In that year, however, the national assembly of the community of the realm which up till then had met as one house, as was the case in Scotland right down to the Union with England in 1707, was divided into an upper and lower house, the latter being on a representative basis as in the case of the House of Commons in England with its knights representing the nobility of the Shires, and the upper being made up of people *personally* entitled to attend the parliament. The *comites* and *barones* who were originally functionaries of the court and the administration were now created a hereditary titled *peerage* nobility.

Side by side with this evolution of the Hungarian feudal nobility from an allodial basis resting on tribal conquest we get the evolution of heraldry but because of the lateness in the creation of the Hungarian nation in Europe, and its easterly position, heraldry came late, and so its nobility had already become fully organised before heraldry had been widely accepted by it. Arms may have begun to be adopted in Hungary earlier than the end of the fourteenth century, but it is really to that period that we must look for their general adoption. The Hungarian nobles who accompanied Sigismund of Luxemburg, King of Hungary and Holy Roman Emperor, to the Council of Constance saw the arms of foreign nobles displayed above their dwellings in Constance, and they thereupon asked Sigismund for permission to assume similar *tesserae nobilitatis*. At first the greater nobles adopted prescriptively their own arms, but after 1400, especially those close to the Court, asked for letters patent.

In ultimate practice the heraldic authorities in Hungary had to deal with :—arms which had arisen prescriptively, and were claimed as appertaining to all members of a particular tribal community, which had retained its original identity, all members of which claimed the

[1] *Scots Heraldry*, 2nd Edition. Oliver & Boyd, Edinburgh, p. 22.

use of its arms ; and arms of those who had become feudalised, whether they had their arms prescriptively or by concession from the Crown, and which were matriculated in the heraldic registers. It should, however, be noted, that while arms were conferred by the Hungarian Crown, as we have seen in the case of Austria with which country it was closely linked, upon citizens, arms could only be *matriculated* or *confirmed*, that is enrolled, as distinct from conferred by the Crown, where the petitioner was already noble. He had to show that he had them either by original letters patent which displayed those arms, or could prove 100 years continuous noble use of the arms. *In other words arms were not confirmed to non-nobles.* On the other hand nobility could be matriculated or confirmed to a petitioner without any actual submission of arms—since for so long in Hungary nobility had existed quite independent of arms. This procedure has something analogous to the Scottish procedure of recording descents in the *Register of Genealogies*, as distinct from the recording of arms and pedigrees in the *Public Register of All Arms and Bearings in Scotland.*

It will, however, be observed that while arms became clearly a *fief of arms* among nobility whose creation had been by letters patent, and must also have so become for those whose nobility was older but who had recorded their arms in their own names and those of their houses, and so submitted to the feudalisation of arms, there were still the individual groups who claimed to be nobles descended from the original noble tribes. These use a common coat of the tribe without any differences whatsoever.

It is evident, since these arms do not serve the purpose for which heraldry was created (which was to differentiate individuals on the battlefield when enclosed in armour, for the banners of magnates themselves to show *their* own *individual* positions on the battlefield, and not that of every member of their family to the ultimate degree, and for warranting documents in the form of seals) it is clear that such arms do not fit into the pattern of noble arms as generally accepted by the Law of Arms. But since their tribal members claim to be noble, and are so accepted in their own country and by their Crown, it is quite clear that such arms have to be accepted as arms indicating nobility. Should, however, these arms come to be matriculated outside of their own realm, then they will have to submit to the feudalisation which that realm's administration of the Law of Arms must insist upon. Consequently, such arms would have to be indi-vidualised to a particular family, its immediate ancestors, relations and descendants. This would be done by differencing, which would be merely completing the evolution of the feudalisation of arms which had begun in Hungary but had not been completed in all cases owing to the late stage at which heraldry had become imposed upon the country. As they are at present, such tribal arms in Hungary would seem to be little better than the plant badges of highland clans, all of which claim to be noble corporations.[1]

In Poland we get a position not unlike, in some respects, the situation in Hungary. Here the whole of the nobility were equal, and titles for any particular noble families were resisted on the score that it destroyed the basic equality which exists among all the noblesse. An echo of which in other lands was the right of a mere noble to call out a duke in a duel, or to enter into a marriage with his daughter, if the opportunity arose, without its being refused as a misalliance.

The nobles of Poland were composed of noble families as elsewhere, and in some cases, as in Hungary, of noble clans. The Polish nobility appear to have been of Scandinavian origin, and this is borne out by the fact that their arms are often composed of runic characters. As a consequence the nobility were indeed a caste, and this made ennoblement from below difficult for some considerable time. It ensured that the plebeians were discouraged in any way from pretend-ing to the attributes of nobility. Consequently, arms were not adopted by non-noble burgesses, whatever might, from time to time, have been the case in adjacent Germanic territories.

Turning to the western Celtic fringe of Europe we come to some-what parallel conditions. We have the overrunning by feudalism of an allodial society, in which lands were held tribally. We have also the fact that all the tribe claimed to be of common blood, although as we suspect is also the case in Hungary, this tended to overlook the serfs and slaves who had been absorbed into its community and could

---

[1] I am very much indebted to Professor Geza Grosschmid of Visegrad, K.M., K.C.M.M., K.C.N., for his assistance in compiling the foregoing account of Hungarian arms.

not really be considered of the same blood as the warrior class who formed the effective element of the tribe or clan. Sooner or later these clan communities whether in Scotland, Wales or Ireland had to submit to Kings who were the heads of a feudal society. Where they could the Crowns attempted to tie down the chiefs of the clans to a terrain, or in Gaelic a *duthus*, which was often incorporated into the feudal society as a barony, or some fief of an existing barony. Where this was not done then the chief in himself, as a captain of a tribe, was brought within the feudal structure and by his fief of arms, which was matriculated in the Lyon Court, in the case of Scotland, with which for the moment we are principally concerned, he was brought into feudal relationship with his superior, whose vassal he became. The present Lord Lyon King of Arms has written fully on this subject, with considerable conviction, and therefore it is not necessary here to elaborate the details, or go over them further.[1]

We have thus a tribe feudalised, or, in terms of its lands, a *duthus*, an allod, feudalised, and we have only to consider the relationship of members of that society, the clan, to its chief, in terms of nobility and the right to arms.

Although we know that every individual of the clan claims to be a gentleman and a noble, we know, in fact, that neither the chiefs nor the Crown accepted this claim. For the tribal society itself was divided into the gentry, the *duine-uasails*, and the plebeians. The former led their men in battle, and formed the council and officers of the Chief's household and tribal organisation. Consequently, although the plebeians may in some clans bear exactly the same surnames as their gentry, there is no question of their automatically being allowed the arms. We suspect that tribal society, presented with identical circumstances of feudalisation, must have been faced with the same situation whether in Scotland or Hungary. Consequently, we have some doubt whether all those who may claim to be tribally noble in Hungary are any more noble than the average Macdonald or MacBean who makes the same claim.

The Celtic tribal society of Scotland having been feudalised in its

[1] See *Scots Heraldry*, Edinburgh, 1956. *The Clans, Septs and Regiments of the Scottish Highlands*, Edinburgh, 1955. *Tartans of the Clans and Families of Scotland*, Edinburgh, 1952.

relation to the Crown through its chief, with his fief of arms, became subject to the Laws of Arms just as much as the Anglo-Saxon and Norman elements of Scotland in the lowlands. Consequently, all clansmen who wish to have arms, have to prove their descent from the eponymous of the tribe, and so their relationship to the chief, and receive their differenced version of the arms. Where they cannot prove that descent, but have such a status that they can be considered noble by descent or else by their office, they are entitled to sue for the chiefly arms, *indeterminately* differenced to show their basic relationship to the chiefly house, without indicating which branch they may come from. Others of the name, who cannot establish reasonable descent from the chiefly house, even indeterminately, then have to sue, provided they have the status to entitle them to petition, for arms on an entirely different footing as though they were strangers in blood. But because they bear the name of the chief, or one of the septs of the clan, they would receive arms which would have some reference to the principal charges in the chief's arms.

For the commonalty of the clan, whether they bear the chiefly surname or not, there is the clan plant badge to which all are entitled, and in addition the chief's badge or crest used as a badge, which is borne within a strap and buckle. Consequently, for anyone who can own a chief, and that is a large part of the population of Scotland, highland or lowland, there is no need to purloin the tribal or chiefly arms, nor to make up bogus arms for themselves, since insignia distinctive to their name can be used, in either the plant badge or the strap and buckle badge as they choose. In addition to which there is the clan uniform or livery provided by its tartan.

When we turn to Welsh heraldry we find a system which is not unlike that of the highlanders of Scotland. We have, first of all, a pre-existing Celtic nation, divided into tribes, but each with their magnates and gentry, and basing their gentility on their descent from ancient noble ancestors, leaders of these tribal formations. Impinging on this came the settlement of Anglo-Normans, many of whom became absorbed by the native civilisation. When arms became general the latter displayed on their arms charges which were unrelated to those of the tribal society of the principalities of Wales even when they had adopted Welsh names. The native Welsh nobles, on the other hand, were tribally organised, and so a deliberate creation of arms for the eponymous was made by the old Welsh bards skilled in heraldry. As a result of this all the branches of a scattered tribe could share in the arms of this ancient, often mythical, chief from whom they claimed to derive their descent. In a large number of cases these original arms assigned to the eponymous are differenced for the various branches. In some cases distinct branches arose, and had already adopted quite different arms from those of their kin, before this conscious effort to tribalise the arms had occurred. In such cases these quite distinct arms were sometimes continued, and they were often enough differenced for their own sub-branches.

It will thus be seen that nobility existed in Wales from an ancient period, and before arms were in use, and that a Welshman's status depended on his gentility of blood, in being descended from one of the ancient Prince-Chiefs, or lesser Chiefs, of one of the Welsh principalities. There was no question of all the people who formed the following of such Chief being, *per se*, noble, as actual descent from the Chief had to be made out.

Those descended from the vulgar of the Welsh civilisation, or who could not make out their ancestry because it was lost in antiquity through defective records, had to assume and, later, obtain a con- firmation or grant of quite distinct arms from any of those of the tribal groups of arms.

Having created the fiction, for practical nobiliary reasons, that an ancestor, who might have lived in some cases before the Christian era, had arms (which were probably those of his best known descendant when arms came to be adopted in Wales) it was possible in a vast number of cases to allot cadet arms to all the rest of the gentry derived from the nobles of that original tribal chiefly family. This is exactly in its final results the same arrangement as we find in Gaelic Scotland, or indeed, in the lowlands too, or in France and elsewhere in feudal Europe, where the *Chief of Name* means the bearer of the undifferenced arms. The failure of the Welsh to perpetuate clan-names as the common names of the people meant that the clan system itself died out, and no tribal organisation survived. All trace of it has disappeared except so far as gentry, often of very different surnames, came to perpetuate their relationship to one another by the similarity of their arms to each other's. All of the arms of such a group show their common relationship to the principal family known to be descended from some well-known princely or chiefly hero of the earlier times. If the clan system had survived, the head of such a principal family would have been formally recognised as the Chief.

It will be observed that both the Scottish and Welsh conception of arms as belonging to those having gentility of blood (ancient nobility) are fundamentally at one.[1]

If we turn to Ireland we have the same basic, clan or tribal, foundation of society. There is the same intrusion of Anglo-Norman settlers of non-Celtic provenance, with their own armorial bearings, and the same ennoblement by grant of arms to later Irish of no known ancient gentility.

The Chiefs of the Irish tribal organisation as a result of Anglo-Norman influence, came to be possessed of arms, as did the chieftains of their branch clans. All, eventually, became subjected to the authority of the government located in Dublin, as the Crown of Ireland, a united Crown with that of England, and under the jurisdiction of the Irish King of Arms, Ulster. The same Laws of Arms, and the same practice of heraldry became established in Ireland as in England. It is the same law that has been administered since. The only variation of practice from that of England is that the Principal Herald of Ireland (whether *Ulster*, or as now under the Republic the Chief Herald, *Priomh-Aralt nahÉireann*) has continued to make confirmations of arms, where a certain length of user can be demonstrated. This practice is no longer followed in England,[2] although it is still in Scotland.

It is therefore certain that arms in Ireland, as in England and Scotland, as we demonstrated earlier, and since have done above in our brief description of Welsh heraldry, are cognizances of gentry, only to

---

[1] The reader's attention is drawn to two important articles on Welsh heraldry by Major Francis Jones, T.D., F.S.A., in *The Coat of Arms*, Vol. V, No. 33, Jan. 1958, p. 349 ; and Vol. V, No. 34, April 1958, p. 9.

[2] The English heralds have the right of confirmation but do not exercise it.

be borne by nobles. As such they can only be borne undifferenced by the chief of any family, whether it is one of Name, comprehending many branches, or some minor, individual family. The funeral certificates of the Ulster Office, as we have shown in *Heraldic Cadency*,[1] make it quite clear that in Ireland cadency was employed as it was in England, Scotland, France and elsewhere. Consequently, we think there is no substance whatsoever in a recent attempt to show that Irish heraldry is quite different from that of England. That all members of an Irish sept (or clan) can use the arms of its chief, is quite erroneous.[2]

Chief Herald of Ireland

To conclude, it would seem that so far as we can see where a tribal society has been overrun by a feudal, or is otherwise in contact with feudalism, the Laws of Arms have come to be substantially the same as in the feudal society, except that instead of a multitude of different and unrelated arms in a given region, there will be a strong tendency for many gentle families to have their own versions of the basic stock arms. In so far as this actual differentiation of " stock " arms did not occur in Hungary to the same extent, it is explicable on the basis that heraldry came late to that country and that the full development and feudalisation of arms was not able to be completed.

One point which should be stressed, is to endorse fully the statement of Major Francis Jones [3] on Welsh tribal heraldry, and that is that *gentility* in Celtic society rested on genealogical descent and ancestry. This is patently true in all the societies we have been discussing. The device of ennoblement (by grant of arms, or otherwise) and the creation of *nobles by letters patent*, or *gentlemen of coat-armour*, is a device of feudalism, originating in a non-tribal society, and eventually forced on the tribal society by feudalisation. In a purely clan society, where

[1] Now being published by Faber & Faber, London, 1961.

[2] Edward MacLysaght, *Irish Families. Their Names, Arms and Origin*, Hodges, Figgis & Co., Dublin, 1957, which we have reviewed fully on this aspect of Dr. MacLysaght's theory in *Duquesne Review*, Duquesne University, Pittsburgh, Penn., Fall Number, 1958, pp. 45 ff.

[3] Major Francis Jones, *op. cit.*

all rank is under God, and inherited, there is no means such as this whereby the ignoble can rise into the noble class by pacific means. Even in the Church all offices, of abbot, prior, bishop and even parson were hereditary, as a study of Highland history in Scotland will show.[1]

[1] Innes of Learney (and Frank Adam), *The Clans, Septs and Regiments of the Scottish Highlands* 1955, pp. 21 ff.

CHAPTER X

THE STATUS OF ARMS OF PATRICIANS, CITIZENRY AND BURGHERS, OF THE CONTINENT OF EUROPE

WHILE we have repudiated any conception that legitimate arms which *could be defended in a court of law* could ever be adopted indiscriminately by people of any status, including the lowest grades of society, we do not exclude non-nobles from the use of arms, when we come to the question of civilian arms.

These have to be considered in two categories, arms where they had only the limited sanction of the civic authority or the custom of the burgh, or of the burghers ; and arms, although civic in origin, which had the ratification of some higher, nobiliary power, or were, at least, accepted by it as equivalent or comparable to noble arms.

As the feudal nobility came to have arms in the surrounding provinces, there is no doubt that in certain countries, such as Germany, Hungary and the Low Countries, and in Italy, to mention the most obvious instances, prominent citizens began taking to themselves ensigns which were armorial in form. In states where the nobility was relatively weak and the cities strong, this could be done with greater impunity than where the cities were weak. Consequently, in Scotland and England, small states, relatively highly centralised, with only a few cities, and most of them dominated by the surrounding gentry,[1] the citizens were never able to establish any independent right to

---

[1] There is ample evidence of this in any study of local history. In Cornwall, for instance, the boroughs had gentry invariably on their councils, and in Scotland, such as at Tain, to take a specific example, the gentry of the names of Ross and McCulloch always provided hereditary officers. See remarks on this in *Gayre's Booke*, Vol. III, 1954 p. 71 ; and W. MacGill, *Old Ross-Shire and Scotland*, Inverness, 1909.

arms arising from the authority or status of being citizens, and based
upon prescriptive rights.   Conversely, neither were they treated in
respect of arms (when they came to need them) as of a different species
of being from the nobility provided their way of life was equivalent to
that of the gentry.

As far as England is concerned it is no doubt true to say that this
development was aided by the decimation of the old nobility by the
Wars of the Roses.   Their ranks were recruited from new nobles, often
of citizenry origin.   This led to a blurring, to some extent, of the
sharp distinction between noble and citizen, and led in its turn to its
being possible for cadets of noble houses to become citizens.   Consequently, when the Visitations became necessary the cities had to be
" visited " as much as the shires.   From this it followed that if one
citizen who was a cadet of a noble house, but who was landless, had
arms, then a citizen of equal *social* standing had a good case to sue
for arms, despite having no feudal fief.[1]   Consequently the same type of
arms were allowed to him if he was considered worthy in his status,
since the Kings of Arms saw no reason to allow an altogether different
species of arms.   Thus, citizens without any fief became ennobled by
the letters patent of arms, and the fief came to reside in the arms
themselves.[2]   At the same time any idea that citizens, *qua citizens*,
could create their own arms and maintain them independently of the
heralds was not tolerated.

In the Low Countries, for instance, quite a different evolution
occurred.   Rich citizens simply made up their own arms (by prescriptive
right) and by the consent of the society in which they lived, and these
appear on their houses, in their stained glass, and on their monuments.

---

[1] There is no doubt that even earlier than the Visitation period of the sixteenth and seventeenth centuries citizens had petitioned successfully for arms and ennoblement, the case of Arnold
and Grimond de Bordeu(x), 1444, being an example of this.   But these earlier ones would be
more difficult to obtain, and often for special services rendered to the Crown as in this case
where it says *ad bona et gratuita servitia*, for good and voluntary service.   Often too they would
be because a fief was being acquired, and ennoblement was a necessary prerequisite.

[2] As the society was feudalised, and still is so far as arms and titles are concerned, which
are held of the Crown, where no landed fief exists, the arms must be the incorporal fief.   This
is undoubtedly so in Scotland (See Innes of Learney, *Scots Heraldry* 2nd Edition, pp. 83 and
121) and we do not think that we can escape the same conclusion so far as English armory is
concerned either.

But not one of these coats was taken cognizance of by the Sovereign's heralds, or recorded then, or now, among the arms recognised by the state and the nobility,[1] unless their descendants have become ennobled. They have remained as simply unrecognised burghal arms. In such an instance we have a case where the city is a powerful unit, and an allod rather than a feudal fief of the Sovereign. In time it comes, perforce, to accept his jurisdiction, but maintains many of its own rights and privileges. Its citizens, although they are subjects of the Prince, are a part of that burghal institution, and they hold shares in the former allod, which has now become partially feudalised, and just as the city has taken to itself its own arms in ancient times, so they have taken their own within the city as part of the same allod, and by the rights which that allod permits, without reference to any external feudal power, such as the Prince.

As we see it the arms of Holland would appear to have developed into the categories which we may summarise as :—

(I) *noble-arms*, recognised by nobility and Crown.

(II) *ancient patrician* arms, of old ruling families of the cities. Taken prescriptively, these families mainly foundered under the Dutch Republic and the Reformation. They may well have been the link between *civilian* and *noble* arms, as we shall see shortly they have been in Italy. The lack of this bridge has caused non-noble heraldry to develop on different lines than it might otherwise have done.

(III) Later *patriciate burgher arms*. The well-to-do citizenry who replaced the patrician, and held *noble* offices in the cities (such as those of sheriffs etc.). These had to use arms for their seals and so assumed them prescriptively. They were new *patricians* even if they were recruited from ordinary freemen of the cities. However, as many of these families became noble on the creation of the monarchy, and their arms were confirmed (*circa* 1815), there was no purely distinctive patrician class left which could demand for itself recognition as the equivalent of noblesse. It would seem the new patricians could no more form a bridge between the nobles and the citizens any more than could the old patricians. The consequence of this is that in Holland, in contrast to Italy, there is no recognition of the rank of patrician as a nobiliary one.

---

[1] For an account of Dutch heraldry see C. Pama, *The Coat of Arms*, Vol. IV, No. 31, 1957, pp. 260 ff.

H

(IV) Non-patrician citizens also took arms to themselves prescriptively. Because there was no *nobiliary* patriciate to oppose them as a body, and as the cities were not feudalised, the use of shields of arms spread throughout the capitalist classes of these trading communities.

Of all these types of arms only those under (I) above are recognised by the sovereign, and only (II) could ever have been classified as *alt bürgher adel*, or (III) *burgher adel*, and (IV) are only, at the best, wappenbürger arms, of no nobiliary significance outside of their towns (or since Holland is a network of trading communities outside of the citizenry classes of Holland). These latter arms have no rights of recognition before any court even as Wappenbürger arms, although since they are such *de facto*, they can be more conveniently so classified than as anything else.

In Italy the city-states were original sovereign states in their own right, and had in some cases under them certain other cities. Bergamo, for instance, was tributary of Venice. In these states they had their own nobility, called the *patricians*, who were equated in every respect with the feudal nobility in the provinces. Often they were cadets of such nobility. Such patricians bore arms *ab immemorabile*.

As a consequence of this a bridge was established in the Italian interpretation of the Laws of Arms between arms of civic families and feudal noblesse. A situation not unlike that in Britain arose. The arms of patricians of the cities were recorded by the monarchies equally with those of the nobility, and no fundamental distinction was made between them when the cities came under these sovereigns.

Thus, in the law of Tuscany it was laid down that all family trees and arms of patricians and nobles had to be recorded in the heraldic registers,[1] while in the codes of Italian nobiliary law we find that the patricians and nobility are taken as equivalent to each other, specifically, for instance, in the cases of Amalfi,[2] Sulmona,[3] Genoa,[4] Bologna,[5] Rome,[6] and others. Furthermore, in the *Fundamental Statutes of*

---

[1] G. Degli Azzi and G. Cecchini, *Codice Nobiliare Araldico*, Florence, 1928, p. 129.
[2] *Codice Nobiliare Araldico*, by G. Degli Azzi and G. Cecchini, Firenze, 1928, p. 85.
[3] *Ut supra*, p. 83.
[4] *Ut supra*, p. 91.
[5] *Ut supra*, p. 147.
[6] *Ut supra*, p. 147.

the Kingdom of Italy of 1848, it is made quite clear that patricians of recognised cities are nobility.[1]

It is the custom in Italy for every noble coat of arms to be surmounted by a coronet, and, as a consequence, because patricians are ranked as nobles, they also are allowed a gold circlet.[2] (See the accompanying figures showing Italian coronets.)

Coronets of Nobles in Italy

The partician class was recruited from the wealthier merchant classes. The steps in such promotion lay in :—first, obtaining the freedom of the city ; secondly, gaining minor offices in civic affairs ; and finally (perhaps 50 years later) rising to the occupancy of those which were reckoned noble charges. Such persons in

Coronets of Patricians in Italy

the process of this social advancement had reached a mode of life, for at least three generations, which was reckoned as living in a genteel manner (*more nobilium*), and, in some cases had already begun inter-marrying with the patricians. If they had not already assumed arms before, they certainly did so at this stage, and they were then admitted to the patrician council,[3] their arms and names enrolled in the registers (Golden Books) officially kept by the Town Clerk or Chancellor, and sometimes painted or sculptured in the City Hall and in other public places.[4] The arms of these patricians were accepted as *de facto* in

[1] *Bolletino Ufficiale de Corpo della Nobiltà*, Italiana, *Organo del Consiglio Araldico Nazionale e della Giunta Araldica Centrale*, Naples, April, 1958, p. 12.

[2] Patricians of Venice were allowed a coronet of 8 flowers (5 visible) alternating with 8 pearls (4 visible) : in recent years it has become the practice to allow this coronet to all patricians instead of the plain circlet.

[3] It should be realised that the whole of civic government in the Italian cities was vested in the *patrician council*.

[4] J. A. Goodall, *Heraldry in Italy during the Middle Ages and Renaissance, The Coat of Arms*, Vol. V, No. 37, Jan. 1959, p.150, says that after the disturbance of the Noble factions in Florence in the thirteenth century possession of nobility was a bar to public office, and that the surviving seals show that in the second half of that century in Florence, Lucca and Siena the " practice of commerce was no bar to the bearing of arms ". We think here that there are two misconceptions. Civic nobility (patricians) did practice commerce (as distinct from feudal nobility) and so this fact alone is no indication of the class involved. Secondly, office was patrician-noble, and so those freemen (merchants) of substantial standing in the cities who succeeded to such offices adopted arms and became patrician-nobles, as we have indicated already. They had arms as new-made *patricians* and not as merchants.

social intercourse, and accepted as *legal* by the order of Malta, Constantinian St. George, St. Stephen, and others, when they were submitted as part of the *proofs of nobility* for admission.

It naturally follows from what we have said that many families of a genteel way of life must have become bearers of self-assumed arms before they were yet admitted to the council of patricians. Such persons, at that stage, were the equivalent of those burgher families of Holland, and elsewhere, who had arms of their own creation which were not recognised as noble, either by the landed feudal nobility or by the sovereign by whom they eventually came to be ruled.

In Italy, with a broadening of civic representation on the councils, on the one hand, which made an aspiration to patrician rank no longer a necessity, and with the passing of these city-states under the Crown, on the other, there came an end to the creation of new patricians. As a result persons of a genteel way of life in the cities, who were what we may call patricians *in embryo*, became fixed in a non-advancing class of citizens. They

Badge of St. Stephen of Tuscany

had, however, already pretended to arms, but there was no way of regularising these arms by being matriculated as patricians. At this stage in Italy the princes under whom the cities passed could have ignored such arms of citizenry (as in some places burgher arms have been) as being of no account or value.

Instead, however, if we consult the regulations of the Italian heraldic authorities,[1] the acts of the Italian parliaments,[2] and finally the current regulations of the *Bollettino Ufficiale del Corpo della Nobiltà Italiana*,[3] which have been approved by King Umberto II, and are the basis of the acceptance or otherwise of nobiliary status in present

[1] *Codice Nobiliare Araldico, op. cit.*, pp. 12 and 14.

[2] Such as those of Tuscany where legislation is provided for arms of citizenry, *Codice Nobiliare Araldico, op. cit.*, pp.140-141, or those of the later ordinances of the Italian state, such as the law of 1848, Act 30, *Bollettino Ufficiale del Corpo della Nobiltà Italiana, op. cit.*, p. 16.

[3] *Op. cit.* which summarises the existing laws of the Kingdom of Italy, and reaffirms them as the law binding on the nobility.

day republican Italy, we find that a special provision was made for such arms. For instance, among the official registers maintained under the heraldic authorities of the Kingdom and Empire of Italy, were the Golden Book of the Italian Nobility, The Heraldic Book of titled foreigners etc. and also the Heraldic Register of the Arms of Citizens. In this register were kept only the arms of citizens which had been accepted as legal and valid under the law. This law recognised the arms of citizens who were of non-noble families, *but of a distinct civility* (*ma di distinta civilta*), the possession of which arms they could prove from authentic documents and certified reproductions of monuments, and which could be established to have been in public and peaceful use for not less than 60 years.[1]

Here then, we have a situation in which it is recognised that prescriptively arms might have arisen among leading citizens of a genteel mode of life, who were not enjoying actual nobiliary rank (from the feudal noblesse of the surrounding province) nor had been inscribed in the Golden Book of the city as patricians which would have made them the equivalent of nobles within the city, but who by their carriage, and way of life, had achieved an advancement over the mass of the citizenry who were not of *distinct civility*. Furthermore, it should be observed that the laws which dealt with the enregistration of these arms in the registers of the heraldic officers of the kingdom were the *Ordinamento dello Stato Nobiliare Italiano*. Consequently, when an Act to control Nobility includes legislation for the control of arms of citizens of proved and *distinct civility* (although it may in the same act clearly call such arms non-noble) it is difficult to avoid concluding that such persons form some kind of *quasi-nobility*. In fact, although they are not *nobiles minores* they are a kind of *nobilitas minima*.

We find from Diego de Valera (1412-1486) in his *Tratado de Nobleza e Fidalguia*, which was published in 1441, that in Portugal there were recognised four modes of acquiring arms—by inheritance : by conquest in war ; by concession from the Prince : and as found among burghers of important towns, rich territories and powerful

---

[1] This Register, *Libro araldico della Cittadinanza*, under the decree of 1896, was also to record, besides their arms, any designations or other distinctions (*o di altri distinzioni*). *Codice Nobiliare Araldico, op. cit.*, pp. 12 and 14.

merchants. But it will be observed that such acquisitions by burghers were by rich and powerful ones. It does not say that all citizens took arms. Since all the higher offices in the cities, of mayors and sheriffs, Chancellors or Town Clerks, were all noble offices the probability is that all these persons took arms in respect of their offices.

When we turn to France we find that there were bourgeois arms of the character of those with which we are dealing. (We are not concerned with self-assumed arms by taverners or moneylenders, and used as tradesmen's seals or as trade signs.[1] Here we are only concerned with those arms which were borne and recorded officially, as in Italy, either by local bodies or the royal officers.)

The evidence is that the French burgesses were adopting arms in the thirteenth century, and this was considered so much an invasion of the privileges of the noblesse and the sovereign, that Philip III, the Hardy, issued a decree in 1283 forbidding them to use arms. Therefore, it is quite clear self-assumed burghal arms were illegal. The case usually cited in support of the right of citizens to arms is that of the citizens of Paris a century later, in the time of Charles V. We think that this example hardly establishes that view at all, but the contrary, as we shall see on further consideration.

L'Oseau, in his *Des Ordres des gentils-hommes*, cap. 5, quoted by Sir George Mackenzie of Rosehaugh [2] in the following words says—

> Gentlemen did not adorn their Atchievements with Helmets, till they found that the Burgesses of Paris, did by warrand from Charles V bear Coat-armours : Whereup, to distinguish themselves from those, Gentlemen did assume Helmets ; and by the 200 Article of the Statutes of Orleance, all who were not Gentlemen by birth, were discharg'd to bear Helmets on their Arms.

From this it is clear that these burghal arms were borne by authority. Furthermore it will also be observed that it would seem that originally the placing of a helm came to signify ancient noble descent—gentry.[3]

---

[1] Some, quoting Mathreu and Galbreath, make the allegation that in France armorial bearings were borne by merchants, including Jews, from as early as 1250 or thereabouts, as well as taverners from about 1400 and workmen from 1450. Furthermore, it is alleged that these have been transmitted to descendants and regularly differenced.

[2] *The Science of Heraldry*. Edinburgh, 1680, p. 87.

[3] In the North-East of Scotland in the seventeenth century arms of ancient families on tomb-stones will be found surmounted of a helm without necessarily displaying a crest, in order to show that they claimed to be noble by ancestral descent, which confirms this interpretation that the helm was not allowed to the *anobli*. *Gayre's Booke*, Vol. III, pp. 75-76.

After some generations it was found that the armigerous burgesses of Paris began to adopt helms over their shields. There can be little doubt that it was done on the ground that they had now become tantamount to established nobles by the passage of the prescribed generations. For in France the ennobled person, in contrast to the practice in Britain, was never considered a noble and was called an *anobli*. The same thing was true in Germany, and ennoblement often meant that the new-man had to abandon his former class and was not accepted by the new one in which his grandchildren only would be completely accepted. From the fact that the arms of citizens in Paris went through the process of being arms without helms (that is like those of anobli) and then assumed helms (as arms of nobles) there seems little doubt that the allowance of arms to these Parisians was of a regular nature. Except that in Britain ennoblement did not involve being classed as an anobli without a helm, it would seem that these arms were quite as valid as those allowed to prominent citizens of London, even if there seems to be some doubt as to their noble status as distinct from burghal, civil or patrician.

The French kings, whose authority was relatively weak, unlike that of the highly centralised English monarchy, had, frequently, to buy the favours of their subjects. This is seen not only in this concession to the citizens of Paris (which was confirmed by some of Charles V's successors), but also by the ennoblement of whole corporations and even counties in the provinces. There is no doubt that it devalued very seriously the currency of arms and nobility, but, nevertheless, it would seem that in French law for all that these arms, and, where nobility was also conceded, the ennoblement which went with them, were genuine enough. The multiplicity of comtes, vicomtes and barons in France at one period or another is another indication of the same debasement of currency in nobiliary ranks—the average count and even marquis or duke, having less status and power than the old English squire or Scottish laird. Nevertheless he is still a count, a marquis or a duke.

That this is a safe conclusion is evident from the fact that Henry III considered this permission to the citizens of Paris, *per se*, to qualify for arms as an abuse since he rescinded the former legislation and limited their bestowal to the mayor and sheriffs. This made the law conform to nobiliary law once more which teaches that wealth of merchandising does not form a basis for admission to nobility and arms, but only service of the weal-public, and by honourable office. Mayors and sheriffs are personally noble and so entitled to arms.

A point which has been made is that at the time of the Edict of 1696 for the matriculation of arms in France arms of families of bourgeois background or origin were recorded. What is overlooked is that burghers had by that time so frequently held noble offices in the magistracy and elsewhere that they were often entitled to be ranked with the feudal nobility and to record arms. Mayors of the third generation to hold the magistracy were granted noblesse.[1]

Nevertheless, while many of the burghers would have been entitled to arms on the grounds we have just cited, we readily admit that it is unlikely that all of them could have qualified on the grounds of holding noble offices for several generations. This edict of November 1696, in the reign of Louis XIV, which promulgated the decree for the creation of a general public armory of the realm, was connected with certain peculiar circumstances. As Dr. Jacques Descheemaeker[2] has pointed out the reason for this register was solely for the fiscal purpose of raising revenue for the prosecution of war ! Consequently, it must be looked upon as very questionable, as a precedent, even in France, on which to ground the value of arms. However, the fact of the matter is that more than 60,000 arms were registered by d'Hozier, the French heraldic officer, and of these as many as 52,000 appear to be those of people of burgher status[3]—although as we have indicated some of them must have qualified for arms by reason of their holding, or their forebears having held, noble civic appointments.

That this was an abuse, solely for revenue-raising purposes, is made

---

[1] This concept was in line with the edict of 1600 of Henry IV which granted nobility to officers who were of the third generation who had twenty years' service. Other variants of the same type of admission to the nobility occur in France. Louis XIII demanded that Petitioners should have the cross of St. Louis and four generations of service, and Napoleon four generations of the Legion of Honour.

[2] Jacques Descheemaeker, Le Droit des Armoiries. *La Vie Judiciaire*, 7-12, March 1960, p. 4.

[3] Jacques Descheemaeker, *Ut supra*.

clear from the fact that, later, Louis XV, in his Ordinance of the 29th July 1760, declared that arms were limited to the nobles and the greater burgesses. By this decree it is evident that the King sought to restore arms in France to their earlier values (so far as the Crown was concerned and the evaluation of them elsewhere) by admitting arms to be only of a noble status or failing that of recognised civility.

As far as Paris was involved the King was in part, at any rate, thwarted by the Parliament of Paris which (no doubt because of the self-interest of the burghers who were using arms which would be declared illegal by that decree) opposed the Monarch and held that his Ordinance was contrary to the law.

While this decree of the Parliament of Paris has considerable bearing on the precedents guiding the use of arms in France today,[1] it has little value in connection with our present study of arms of civility. For, at the most it means that in addition to the arms of nobles and families of high civility, whose arms the Crown was prepared to recognise, there were other arms borne by citizens which the Crown was not prepared to accept, although the Parliament of Paris, apparently, was insisting that it should, at least to the extent that the Crown should not have power to interdict them. Since arms are ensigns of honour and flow from the Fountain of Honour in most realms, if not all, it would seem that this was a clear invasion of the prerogatives of the French Crown by the Parliament of Paris.[2]

The outcome of this, therefore, is that there was in France at the time of the Revolution arms which were those of nobles and civilians

[1] In modern France, without any survival of the former royal control of arms, armorial bearings are protected before the civil courts. The principles involved to prove a right to arms are, primarily, evidence of long use, and no infringement of older arms. To establish long user the record of arms under the Crown and in connection with noble names is accepted by the Courts as conclusive. But there is no law to prevent the assumption of new arms provided that they do not infringe those of other parties. On the other hand such self-assumptive arms are not allowed to carry any helm, crest or coronet. See Jacques Descheemaeker, *La Vie Judiciare*, 29 Feb.-5 March, pp. 1 ff. ; and 7-12 March 1960, pp. 4 ff.

[2] It is significant that at the end of the old regime anyone who wanted arms of status did not assume them prescriptively, but bought a nominal secretaryship of the King. At the time of the Revolution the King had on his establishment in this way 206 secretaries, besides 46 titular or honorary secretaries. Having obtained noble employment the petitioner now became an anobli and armigerous, with arms which had full nobiliary status, not only in France, but in any other realm where they were advanced.

of high status, and in addition a mass of other arms, borne by citizens in Paris, and elsewhere, many of which had found their way into the general enregistration of d'Hozier, and many which probably had not been of record elsewhere, and which conferred no status whatsoever, neither in the eyes of the citizens, nor in those of the Crown. All those, however, who aspired to noble rank, as we have explained elsewhere, still applied for arms to the Crown, and did not in any way consider that the weakness of the Crown's powers to prevent a mass creation of arms left them free to make up their own arms. The status, therefore, of arms in France down to the end of the old regime at the time of the Revolution [1] was that those which the Crown recognised were either noble or of distinct civility, and, presumably the mere fact that arms were on record in d'Hozier's general enregistration of 1696 did not, in itself, confer any status at all—they were looked upon as an indiscretion of a previous reign.

Therefore, although the arms of burgesses in Paris are often cited as examples of the non-nobiliary status of arms in France, they are nothing of the kind. They are examples of the too generous bestowal of honours by the Sovereign at one period, which were later limited by his successors. Consequently, these arms are not on the same footing as the arms of citizenry of distinct civility in Italy.

When we come to the Holy Roman Empire we find, in connection with burgher arms, a situation developed much closer to that of Italy.

Arms in some parts of the Empire were quite late in being assumed by the nobility, as we have seen in the case of Hungary. One outcome of this was that not only did prescriptive assumptions of arms occur, but, later, concessions of arms were made by letters patent from the Crown to the already established noblesse who were without them. Consequently, not only did letters patent of nobility contain nobilitation and arms for the *new man*, but there were needs from time to time to issue letters patent of arms alone as distinct from arms and nobilitation.

[1] Another evidence that recognised arms had a nobiliary status is shown by the fact that on the 23rd June 1791 the Revolution made illegal the use of arms along with liveries, and the titles of Excellency and My Lord. Paul Adam, *De l'Acquisition et du port des Armoires, Recueil du IV*e *Congrès International des Sciences Généalogique et Héraldique*, Brussels, 1958, p. 92.

In other words we get here the concept of letters patent in *forma meliori* and in *forma communi*.[1]

Having that development already to deal with in the nobiliary and armorial offices of the Empire, and having at the same time in parts of the Empire burghers who were patricians, as those in Italy, and in other parts, burghers who had no nobiliary or patrician status but had prescriptively taken arms to themselves as we have seen happened in some Dutch towns, and among citizenry in Italy, it follows that inevitably the Empire was forced to deal with the issue in a three-fold way : *nobility and arms* ; *arms conceded alone* to existing noblesse who were without ; and *arms conceded to those who were neither noblesse nor patricians*.

The famous roll of arms of the mid-sixteenth century of the *Geschlechtergesellschaft " Zur Katze "* in Constance is a case of arms (whether they arose prescriptively or not) which belonged to patrician families who were called *honourable burghers* or *probi cives*. Even so, such patrician families always felt that their social status was enhanced by actual nobilitation, and many of their descendants came to be ranked not as patricians but as nobles. The social distinction is probably that which exists in England between wealthy town-dwellers and those who have a country estate and become what the vulgar call " county ".

The Empire could have ignored the arms of citizenry, as apparently was the case in Holland, but in Austria and Hungary action was taken rather similar to that which has occurred in Italy. But, whereas in Italy the arms of citizenry arose as prescriptive arms, and then came to have a legalised position under the Crown by recording them, in these countries, on the contrary, the Crown itself made the concession, but without conceding at the same time ennoblement with them.

Indeed the letters patent are quite specific and they read—*Wappenbriefer ohne Nobilitation—Letters Patent of Arms without Nobilitation*.[2]

---

[1] This distinction has never had any legal significance in the British realms, since, as we have shown earlier, while the English patents are now in the latter form, they were formerly of the first type. As they are specific in their reference to being in accordance with the Law of Arms it follows that they convey the intent of *in meliori* even if set out *in communi*.

[2] In recent years actual grants of arms have been made in the English College of Arms, which are tantamount to those conferred by the Empire *without nobilitation*. These are the so-called *honorary arms* conferred by the English Kings of Arms upon foreigners. The fact that they do not carry nobiliary status only emphasises the nobiliary character of the normal grant. Innes of Learney, *Scots Heraldry*, p. 92, fn. 2.

Yet these documents were recorded in Vienna in the *Adelsarchiv*, in the office of the Royal and Imperial Minister of the Interior. Once again, therefore, we see, as in the case of citizenry arms in Italy, that while

Helmet of
Citizenry in Italy

they are specifically labelled as non-nobiliary, at the same time they are subject to the legislation and control of the department dealing with *Adel* or Nobiliary affairs. Consequently, this is so much the same as what we find in Italy, on which we have legislation down to the present time, that we must consider the cases identical, and assume that all these grants of non-noble arms to burghers in Austria, and likewise in Hungary, are arms of families of distinct civility—a kind of quasi patrician or noble class, which was socially of some higher status than the ordinary freemen or burgesses in the hierarchies of the principal cities, and whose rank and position was enhanced further from the concession of arms from the Crown. Such people were called *Wappenbürger*: armigerous citizens.

Helmet of
Noble in Italy

However, as in Italy, a distinction is made between their arms and those of the nobles and patricians. In Italy it is the denial of the circlet, and restriction to a steel, closed helmet, without collar and medallion, which means that at the best such arms are permanently frozen in some kind of anobli position, below real or complete nobilitation. In the Empire coronets have been allowed freely to all the noblesse as in Italy and elsewhere.[1] Consequently, in Austria and Hungary the limitation placed on these arms was, as in Italy for similar arms of citizenry, a denial of the coronet of a noble. The helmet which is generally found allowed on such arms is the plain helm, without any garnishings either in silver or gold.

Despite what we have said concerning the denial of the coronet to burghers there are exceptions, such as in that allowed to the family of Geroldt in Munich. But the petition was by Balthaser Geroldt, who

[1] In distinction from the practice in Britain where they are allowed only to peers, chiefs of names, and other leading armigers.

was not only a master builder, but also a Councillor, which meant that he held what, elsewhere, would have been agreed to have been a noble office, and so was noble in his own person.   Consequently, although his arms appear to have been non-noble *Wappenbürger* arms, this concession made in 1558 allowed him insignia which was noble in respect, possibly, of the noble office which he held.

When such families, having achieved this amount of status (sub- or quasi-noble), as was confirmed by such a concession of arms from

Geroldt

Trautwein

Esquire's Helmet
with 1 gold bar

the Crown, wished to advance higher, because they had achieved some landed estates, or succeeded to offices conceded to be personally noble, they had to sue by petition for an augmentation of nobility to their achievement, and for letters of nobilitation.   For instance, in the case of Heinrich Trautwein of Hohenschofen near Hagenau we find him petitioning that his old arms (presumably based on an earlier concession as a Wappenbürger) should be augmented with a *coronet* and that he should be given nobilitation.   In the authorisation we read that the augmentation of the coronet and the grant of the nobility is conceded with a tournament helm.[1]   This latter is the simple type of helm as used in England by esquires and gentlemen with the addition of one bar.   The same type of helm is used in Scotland today for the basic noblesse conferred by the Letters Patent, and so is consistent with this Imperial use at this time and place.

[1] A. C. Fox-Davies, *The Art of Heraldry*, London 1904, p. 430 ; being a translation from A. G. Ströhl.

We can in the light of the foregoing understand why a leading Hungarian authority of the early sixteenth century says that arms are not a *sine qua non* of nobility—" Arms, granted by the sovereign, are not a necessary appendage of nobility, but only its ornament ; for a grant of arms in itself does not make anybody noble, since many citizens and commoners have arms granted by sovereigns, and yet they cannot be counted among the nobles ".[1] Such a statement is strictly true for Austria and Hungary, and some other realms, but it is not of international application, since we have seen that both for Savoy, Portugal, Sweden and the British Isles (where three jurisdictions are concerned), and even for France, the contrary is the case. In view of the progression which can be traced from arms of citizenry to arms of patricians and nobles it is clear that such arms are analogous to those of the Italian citizenry, which confer a degree of status, of *distinct civility*, which distinguishes the owners from not only the proletariat but the rest of the citizens and freemen at large. Furthermore, once all the legislation on the use of such arms comes under the very offices which legislate upon the arms of nobility, and is comprehended under the distinctive local variants of the Laws of Arms, as applied in such realms where these types of arms exist, these arms definitely confer some status on that account alone.

Originally the helm was a prerogative of ancient gentry : but as the rank below always tends to assume that of the one above, it is not surprising to find that in Italy a dexter-facing closed steel helm (without a collar and medallion around the neck) is now allowed to citizenry of distinct civility—whereas nobles have silver open and barred helms, and royalty golden. They are, however, denied crests. Consequently, from the form and metal of the helms, and lack of crest, the arms of citizenry can be distinguished from those of nobility and patricians.

Such arms as these of families of distinct civility (and more so than those of yeomanry in Switzerland, and even burghers of Germany) present a problem for heraldic registration in England, Scotland and Ireland, whenever a cadet of any of these stocks settles within their

---

[1] *Tripartitum of Werbőczi*, 1514. Werbőczi was the first and greatest codifier of Hungarian statutory and common law in the sixteenth century.

bounds, and wishes to record his arms. For these arms are not noble (clearly not so in the case of some German ones the patents of which specifically reserve from the grantee nobilitation) although those of Italian citizenry, being of distinct civility, come very close to being such. It would seem, therefore, that the precedents provided in the Empire, where burgher or landtmann holders of *wappenbriefs* (having achieved the status to claim ennoblement) had to sue for nobilitation and permission to have their ancient arms recorded with their letters patent of nobility, provide the course which should be followed.

Such arms are in the same category as " honorary arms " granted in England, which are clearly understood to have no nobiliary character, and which cannot, as a consequence, be recorded by matriculation in Scotland.[1] They could not be matriculated, as, so far as the Law of Arms is concerned, they are not such arms as the Crown's Commissioners (the Kings of Arms) could take cognizance. Presumably, therefore, they would have to be the subject of a re-grant, provided their bearers had reached the nobiliary status *of virtuous and deserving persons*, when such a grant would confer with it nobilitation. Even so, one would imagine, it would be necessary to make some minor change in the arms so as not to lead to the suggestion that all persons bearing that burgher coat were now ennobled.

[1] Sir Thomas Innes of Learney, *Scots Heraldry*, 2nd Edition, 1956, p. 92, n. 2.

CHAPTER XI

COUNTRYMAN ("PEASANT") NON-NOBLE ARMS ON THE CONTINENT OF EUROPE

THE evidence we have traversed leaves no doubt as to the status of arms in the British Isles. Therefore anything that now follows does not affect that status in any way. Even if all coats of arms outside of the British Isles were actually *tesserae ignobiles*, it would not alter the clear meaning which the law based on actual statutes and precedents establishes for them in Scotland, England and Ireland. Therefore, references which have been made by some writers to so-called peasant and other ignoble arms on the continent of Europe do not affect the issue at all, as to the status of arms in the Britannic realms. In addition to that we think that there has often been a misinterpretation of the facts in these connections.

In the first place it has been pointed out that in Switzerland and in parts of the Low Countries, in the former till the present time, and in the latter during the Middle Ages, there have been peasant families with arms. This word peasant has, however, to be rightly understood. It does not mean what it is used to connote in English—agricultural labourers—but small freeholders. In other words it refers to *yeomanry* in the correct sense of that term.

Now if we look back on the caste structure which arose in Europe as a result of the conquests by Germanic tribes we saw that their leaders became the nobility, and their followers were freeholders of yeomanry status. In most countries, if not all, at first, these latter were recognised as belonging to the frank or free classes, although with time the upper and lower freeman divided, so that in the end the noble did not intermarry with the yeoman. But in some societies this division was not so strongly developed, and in this respect,

Switzerland, because of its own peculiar social history, tended to be a peasant rather than a noble society. It is, therefore, obvious, that when arms became the cognizances of nobility, that these could spread to classes below the noblesse in such societies where the nobility was not numerous, and not powerful enough to prevent that happening. Consequently, arms began to be used, and have continued to be used, by non-noble, but free yeomanry in Switzerland. Such arms are not noble arms, but it would hardly be proper to call them ignoble or plebeian, since they were adopted by petty landowners, holding by free tenure, who had, militarily, to defend their lands, and who, although a yeomanry, or so-called peasant, class, formed what must be considered as some type of sub-*petite noblesse*. Since they often existed in a state of society where there was not a powerful nobility over them, they tended to be more important as a class than they would have been in countries such as England or Scotland.[1]

When we come to the Low Countries where we are told that there were petty landowners who had arms, we are in a society where the nobility was as strongly entrenched as in Britain. But here we have small landowners, holding by free, that is military, tenure, because there had been no success in preventing subinfeudation into such small units. What has happened in such cases is that the general rule which was that below *vavasoria*, the holding of a free feu was not considered ennobling, has been varied by the circumstances of local evolution. As a consequence we have the concept of a free feu entitling to arms (once arms became the insignia of a feudatory) being conceded to a lower degree than would have occurred in many other

---

[1] In Switzerland, it should be realised, there are arms of various kinds, although the frequent reference to peasant arms in Switzerland, and the ease with which anyone can register arms there today, may lead one to assume that all Swiss arms are of these types. In this country there are arms derived from the Empire, from Savoy, and France, from the Pope, and others. Consequently, besides purely " peasant " arms there are arms which belong to *Uradel*—the most ancient nobility of all, and others which belong to high patrician families, especially in such places as Zurich and Berne, whose members ensign their arms with coronets, in order to show that they are nobles. On the other hand there are burgher arms, such as in St. Gall and Basle, and since the sixteenth century such families have placed a closed helmet over their shields. How far all of these are necessarily non-noble, rather than a species of *anobli* would involve research in each case. Where families are of higher burgher status, derived from mayors and sheriffs, and the like, they can scarcely be called non-nobles, since the occupation of such offices have always been held to ennoble.

I

countries. Here, then, we have another instance of the use of arms by people who elsewhere could not have been considered noble, and were not actually noble in their own country, but who had a species of sub-nobility based on the fact that they actually held fiefs, and belonged to the frankish class which had originally conquered the land.[1]

In France we have the same position. In the County of Clermont (Beauvaisis) and the bailiwick of Senlis the arms of merchants, burghers and farmers who *possessed fiefs*, are recorded on heart-shaped shields.[2]

Khün

Furthermore, in the same rolls of the Empire Office of Arms which contain *Wappenbürger* arms we find the concession of " peasant " arms. If *nobiliary* status could be distinguished from purely *armorial*, as was done in the case of citizens of standing who received *Wappenbürger* arms, then the way was equally open for giving arms to substantial yeomanry.[3] This was in fact what the Crown actually did. As a result we find, from time to time, in the same records to which we have referred from the *Adelsarchiv* in Vienna, examples of arms to men described in each case as a *Landtman*, in places like the Tyrol. These are just those types of places where a strong, free, and very independent and often martial yeomanry existed. Such a coat was granted in 1546 with helm, mantling, wreath and crest, to George Khün, " ain Landtman in Tyrol ". Such coats, no doubt, acted as a stepping stone to ultimate nobilitation, as we have seen was the case of Wappenbürger arms.

Such peasant arms, of whatever category they may have been, do not destroy the nobilitary status of arms in other realms, and they are to be regarded as exceptions to the general rule, and not the disproof.

---

[1] Even so, it is said that such arms were not allowed to be borne in the normal way on shields, but on heart-shaped shields, to distinguish them from those of the nobles.

[2] Paul Adam, *De l'Acquisition et du Port des Armoires, Recueil du IVe Congrès International des Sciences Généalogique et Héraldique*, Brussels, 1958, pp. 86-87.

[3] Quite apart from the case of peasant arms of yeomen holding petty freeholdings by military service from a very ancient period whose arms had arisen in emulation of their superiors. Because they rested on some kind of free fief, they must have been some species of minute nobility—which we have called sub-noble.

CHAPTER XII

MIT SCHILD UND HELM

WE now come to a matter which is of considerable importance in European heraldry (outside of the British Isles)—the nobiliary significance of the helmet, the type of helmet, or the lack of it in certain realms, at varying periods.

What we are about to explain will show a failure on the part of certain jurisdictions to enforce the Law of Arms completely. But lest we are too loud in our condemnations of such failures we should remember that we have not even found it easy to enforce the whole nobiliary law. Thus while in England and Scotland the heraldic authority has been able to ensure a complete control over arms, the law has been far less successful in controlling the proper use of the nobiliary ranks of gentleman and esquire. It is therefore not surprising that in other states it has sometimes been equally difficult to control the nobiliary use of arms. Curiously enough, in one of these—Belgium—the control of the title of *ecuyer*, right down to the present time, has been saved from the abuse of degradation which the rank of esquire has suffered in the British Isles, while at the same time they have been less successful in restricting the use of arms.

In some states, of which the Empire and France are particularly typical examples, the central authority represented by the Crown was weak, as we have already seen to some extent. This meant that it was often unable to enforce its authority. It also meant that it had in effect, on occasions, to bribe its subjects. Added to that there was often a more than ordinary need for revenue.

The outcome of this situation is seen in France where in 1696 the edict of Louis XIV setting up the general register of arms actually allowed them to anyone paying the necessary fees—since the whole reason for the measure was to raise revenue for purposes of war. The need for revenue guided the Empire's hand in the same direction.

The result of this is that from time to time in France, in the Empire, and in some of the states of the Empire such as Saxony and in the Rhineland we have, in addition to arms of noblesse, and arms of anobli, and of the high burghers (arms ranging from those of civility to patrician in their approximations) other arms which are so far as one can see non-noble. Actually, fewer of these are non-noble than is usually suggested, since many of them are no doubt arms of anobli—that is of persons borne non-noble, and still called non-nobles, but who were occupying noble charges and on the way to establishing their nobility.

Whenever the Crown found itself strong enough to do so, or the nobility were powerful enough to force the hands of the Crown, steps were taken to restrict the rights of non-nobles to arms. As a consequence of this, as we have seen in the case of France, Louis XV took measures in that direction, and the same thing was done by the Austrian Crown both in Austria itself and in the Austrian Netherlands.

Such measures ranged from a denial, often ineffectually, of arms to non-nobles, to a refusal to recognise non-noble arms, even if the burghers were in fact using devices upon shields.

In fact, however, such states had usually to fall back upon the ruling that the arms of nobles bore over them a helmet, with or without a crest. Thus, the Crown tended, in such cases, to retreat from its desired position of denying the burghers shields of arms, and it drew the line of delimitation between arms which were recognised (which were those of nobles, anobli, and high burghers of civility or patrician rank) and which had the helm over them and those which were not recognised, and which had no such additament.

Originally this difference, in France, for instance, had merely been that between the noble and the anobli, (among whom should be put the citizens of Paris who were permitted the use of arms but later these latter came to use the helmet also). At a later stage still in certain states the burghers of approved civility generally began to use helmets.

The use of the helmet thus at one stage became the distinguishing mark between authorised and non-recognised arms.

In the British realms such a distinction never arose, for the Crowns had stood firm on the nobiliary character of arms, and it was never necessary to ensign arms with a helmet to ensure that they were understood to be noble. The fact of the matter is therefore that all armigers in England, Scotland, Ireland, Wales, Man, and the Channel Islands have always been entitled to a helm, and from the sixteenth century to wreath and mantling.

Because of the inability, for one reason or another, to prevent wholesale breaches of the law, it thus came about, for instance, that the only arms recognised by the Crown in some countries were those which were described as *mit Schild und Helm*.

Nevertheless, the pressure for the use of the helmet was very great on the part of those burghers whose arms were unrecognised as having any nobiliary or patrician value at all. This probably accounts for the fact that in Austria, for instance, we get instances, to which we have already alluded, of grants of arms, complete with helmets, wreaths, mantles and crests, which were specifically stated to be without nobility. Although it ought to be remembered that such liberal grants only occurred at certain periods, and the whole trend of subsequent legislation was to prevent such easy acquisition of arms, without nobiliary connotation, and ended, in Austria, in the refusal of arms to non-nobles altogether.

Owing to this pressure for the use of the helmet a stage was reached in some realms when the non-nobles could not be denied the use of a helmet and so we find them being allowed a closed helmet, while an open helmet or one with golden bars was considered the prerogative of the noblesse. Generally speaking, in the Empire, a point was reached in which the barred helmet was looked upon as belonging to the high nobility, and an open one accompanied by a collar to the noblesse in general. These helmets were recognised as belonging to people of tournament rank—whereas the closed helmet was abandoned to other, mainly unauthorised, users of arms. Spener[1] tells us that the exception to this last was in the case of doctors, orators and laureate poets who had the right to the open helm—but in this there is a misunderstanding, since these classes were noble by their occupation. In

---

[1] Insignium theoria, 1717, p. 309.

fact, they were anobli, and so had a right to its use, since the anobli had already by that time become possessed of the open helmet.[1]

This gradual development is seen in a series of edicts. Thus in Loraine, that of 15th September 1577[2] attempted to prevent anoblis using the barred helmet. While in the Low Countries we find the same type of legislation, where, in 1592, Philip II, forbade the use of helmeted arms to non-nobles, and in 1662[3] when Charles IV did the same in Loraine. In Spain in the sixteenth century we have the same kind of thing happening.[4]

In France we find that in 1555 there was a decree of the Parliament of Paris which punished citizens who, being non-noble, used a helmet, or their wives who encircled arms with a cordeliere.[5] The edicts of Orleans, January 1560, of Blois, May 1597 and of March and November 1583 all interdicted non-nobles from using helmets.

Throughout the seventeenth century there were further decrees of the Parliament of Paris, and under the family of d'Hozier, who were hereditary Judges of Arms in France, from 1641 to the Revolution, the principle was established firmly that only titled nobles could have a helm with appropriate coronet, and the untitled had the right to the helmet with silver bars, while, normally the anobli had none. These latter include the long list of categories which are usually cited[6] as evidence that non-nobles, that is plebeians, had the right to arms in France—but as all of these were noble by office, they were in fact anobli and not non-nobles as such.

However, from this, to us, erroneous interpretation of the arms of so-called " non-nobles ", there has sprung the doctrine widely held in France that anyone can take arms as long as he does not ensign them

---

[1] This indicates once more how confused is much of the thinking on this question—these holders of noble employments were personally noble, and so anobli. Yet they are called non-nobles, and from that there then flows a whole argument as to the arms, or the helmets to which certain types of non-nobles are entitled !

[2] Paul Adam, *De l'Acquisition et du port des armoires*, IV⁰ *Congrès International Généalogique et Héraldique*, Brussels, 1958, p. 95, quoting Pelletier, *Nobiliaire de Lorraine*, p. XXXIX.

[3] Paul Adam, *ut supra*, citing F. de Neufchateau : *Rec. des anc. ordonn.*, I. 86.

[4] Paul Adam, *ut supra*, p. 96.

[5] Paul Adam, *ut supra*, p. 90.

[6] Paul Adam, *ut supra*, pp. 91-92.

with a coronet or helm, and it is on this basis that the French Courts, in the absence of any very clear legislation to the contrary, proceed today.

Therefore, in France, arms which are not ensigned with helm, crest or coronet are not noble, nor even anobli at the present time.

Belgium has been considerably influenced by France, and under the Act of the 13th February 1815 the only control is over arms which bear helms,[1] so that in fact the non-noble appear to consider themselves free to bear shields of arms, provided that they are not accompanied by helmet, crest or coronet. In other words the Crown would appear to be only interested in the control of such arms, and, presumably, in legal theory, only these are arms, as was, apparently, the position at an earlier period under the Habsburgs.

While in the countries under French, influence the complete absence of the helmet appears to be the dividing line between recognised noble arms and those of plebeians, in those markedly under German influence the dividing line shows a deeper erosion into the rights of the noblesse. There the point of restriction of the use of arms is at that which concedes the open helmets to the noblesse, and forbids others to bear arms so ensigned. Consequently, a closed helmet, as is normally used in England, Scotland or Ireland would be considered non-noble in Germany !

It will be seen that so far as these countries which we have mentioned, and any others influenced by them, have been concerned, there has been a tendency from time to time towards regarding shields as being the right of anyone to adopt freely. At the same time, it must be remembered, that this apparent general right for anyone to become possessed of a shield solely is, even in these realms, only possible as an interpretation of the nature of arms, by disregarding the very strict legislation which was introduced from time to time, and attempted to be enforced, by the Crowns concerned against such widespread assumptions of arms. That of 1760 in France, fortified by the fact that the French Revolution in 1791 abolished arms with

---

[1] Arendt et de Ridder, *Législation héraldique de Belgique* (1595-1885). As a consequence of this, such works as Armorial Général de Belgique, by Koller et Melia, Brussels, show noble arms with coronets and blazon the crests, and non-noble as shields alone, without any blazon of the crests.

nobiliary titles and liveries, as we have already shown, and the progressively very restrictive legislation in Austria, and right down to 1912
in Saxony,[1] all indicate that such interpretations as to the free right
to arms by anyone as long as they do not take helmets, or where they
do in certain realms restrict themselves to closed ones, are only founded
upon a disregard of such legislation, and the clear intentions of the
Sovereigns in each realm concerned.

Consequently, such precedents cannot be accepted as a basis on
which to estimate the nature of arms in other states (such as Scotland,
England, Ireland, Portugal, Savoy-Italy, etc.) where both the will of
the Fountains of Honour, and the administration of the law, has been
such that these grave abuses of the use of arms have not been allowed.
Indeed, these exceptions to the rule, that arms are of nobiliary connotation, prove that very rule. For we see how in the face of a general
abuse the Crowns in each case (sometimes after creating the abuse
themselves for financial reasons) took repeated steps to put it down.
Where they failed to do that, in order to limit the scope of the abuse,
they chose to regard simple shields, or in some lands shields with
closed helms, as not coming within the scope of their purview. In
other words to the Crowns concerned shields were not armorial
bearings as they understood them.

Much the same difficulty was arising in Portugal and Spain. In
the former country the law was quite explicit against the free adoption
of arms, but, ultimately there began to appear shields which were not
composed of the heraldic metals of gold and silver.

Thus in the *Nobiliario* of Feeran Mexia, 1485, we are told that base
and plebeian people did not use the contrasting tinctures normal in
heraldic blazonry, and he hesitated to call these arms. We have also
the beginnings of the same sort of thing in England, in merchants'
marks, where they began to be placed on shields, and, ultimately,
they were tinctured, sometimes being colour upon colour, although

---

[1] Der Herold, 1914, p. 216. We might here say that we cannot quite see why M. Paul
Adam, when referring to this decree, *ut supra*, p. 98, says that it does not in any way modify
the heraldic law in Germany for the free adoption of arms. Any passing of a law cancelling
any previous practice makes it impossible to say that previous practices, whether they were
lawful or not, are unaffected by it. It would seem to us that that law effectively extinguished
in Saxony any right of free adoption of arms, even if such a legal right existed at all before.

often enough colour on metal or vice versa.[1]   We have also the merchants in England placing heraldic devices outside their shops, red pales, and red crosses, probably on shields, and the like.   But none of these developments, although they were arms of a sort, were reckoned heraldry, and were not recorded as arms.   Nevertheless, so far as Scotland is concerned in daily practice, and so far as England is concerned if the authorities there wish to exercise their authority through the Earl Marshal's Court, all such uses can be suppressed as contrary to the law.

We have, however, drawn attention to these tendencies, as they indicate that even where the law was explicitly administered to maintain the nobiliary character of arms, there was the same struggle to put down the abuse of arms, as there existed in countries under French and German influence.   The only difference being that in the British Realms, in Savoy, in Portugal, and others we have mentioned, the law was administered and triumphed over the abuses, whereas in the others it failed to be entirely successful, and often had to compromise with the abuse, in some degree or another.   In these as a consequence, a coat of arms was nothing if it was not composed of a *Schild und Helm*.

[1] For examples of English marks which take on an heraldic appearance see, E. M. Elmhirst, Merchants' Marks, Harl. Soc., London, 1959, p. 14.

CHAPTER XIII

THE VARIOUS MEANINGS TO BE ATTACHED IN NOBILIARY LAW TO THE TERMS NOBILITY AND GENTRY

WE have had to use the words Noble and Gentle and their related terms frequently in the preceding pages without entering upon any lengthy or precise definition of them, which has been reserved to this place. Already, however, from some of the evidence which has been reviewed, and our comments thereon, some understanding of the two sets of terms may have emerged. Nevertheless, since there is very much misunderstanding and lack of clarity in many people's minds as to the precise meaning of these terms we think that it is advisable to go into them at some length.

At the beginning of this book we talked of a common nobility throughout Central and Western Europe which had come down from the ancient conquests of those lands. Then, from time to time, at the later stages of development, this nobility had been augmented by recruits who were ennobled by the Prince. Later, as we have explained, this was done by grant from the Kings of Arms.

Out of this basic nobility there arose a peerage *as a rank of the nobility*. The higher peers, such as Earls and Counts, with later, Dukes, were in fact in a vast number of cases originally ruling princes themselves who had become absorbed into one large empire of some sort or another, and become subordinate to King or Emperor as a consequence. As a result of this, right down through the post-mediaeval period to our own times, certain Earls in Scotland have been able to style themselves princes with propriety and the support of the whole force of nobiliary law, custom and history behind them. It was not any presumption, for instance, when the Great Marquis in his proclamation styled himself the High and Mighty Prince, James, Marquis of Montrose, etc.

The provincial princes, who often ended as being dukes and earls in someone else's kingdom, had their own great councils, as had the kings and emperors, and to these were called from time to time certain of the nobility as counsellors.

At first the baronies and manors were the same thing—indeed, we will find right down to the Renaissance in Scotland that this was so. (For instance, the barony of Nigg is repeatedly called a manor as often as a free barony.)   However, in England a complication was created by the Norman Conquest. The native English had already the land feudally organised in manors, of varying sizes, the whole of which are listed in the Domesday Book. With the Norman Conquest we find that a very large part of these passed to the conquerors. (Of these it is said[1] there were 700 greater baronies.)   These manors would vary from the great manors to lesser manors dependant upon a single one. The great holdings were subinfeud, and their tenants were barons holding of the greater barons, who were the tenants in chief (*in capite*) of the Crown. Hence a charter of William of Gloucester, in the time of Henry II, which is to *Dapifero suo, et omnibus Baroniis suis*. King John tried ineffectually to stop this practice, which strengthened the position of the greater barons against the Crown in particular, and it was not till the time of Edward I that subinfeudation was stopped in England.

Superimposed on this the Normans evaluated each feu in terms of knight's fee, (called by the Germans *Rittergut*) of which there were about 60,000 in England. A great barony or manor might be worth many knights' fees, while a small one would be only part of a single fee.[2]

There can be little doubt that the barons who rebelled against John and brought him to sign Magna Carta were not only the greater barons, but also the smaller as well, some of them holding in chief, and others of the more powerful feudatories of the Crown.

[1] John E. Cussans, *Handbook of Heraldry*, London, 1882, p. 201 ff.

[2] This type of knighthood, arising from such a fee, is the basis of the eventual knights bachelor in England.

At some stage or another in this evolution of the greater baronage in Norman England a rental of £400 became recognised as the minimum for such lords, and gave them direct access, presumably by right, to the sovereign in council, apart from others whom the Prince may have chosen to help him in his deliberations.

By the time of Henry III there had grown up the practice of calling barons to parliament by writ. In other words the Crown began limiting the right of the greater feudatories to sit automatically in the Sovereign's council as of right, and a selective process which had the merit, from the monarch's point of view, of being at the command of the King began to be put into practice. The people who from then onwards began to form his council, were not only those greater barons who could not be ignored and who could, at first at any rate, demand a writ of summons, but also smaller feudatories, who might not even be tenants *in capite*, but whose advice was helpful to the Sovereign. It may also be mentioned here that it is believed that the holding of fiefs by *grand sergeantry* [1] tended to be a basis for membership of parliament. This may be another way of saying that those whom the Crown favoured were called, since the persons holding by *grand sergeantry* were just those persons and houses particularly favoured by the prince, and, consequently, at first, and for some time afterwards, likely to be most loyal to his cause.

However, the result of all this in England was that the writ became the normal procedure for attending parliament. Ultimately it all ended by affording the privilege of parliament to the heirs of those so writted. Many who had automatically held *per baroniam* no longer were able in right of that alone to be accepted as barons of parliament. By the time of Richard II the practice started of creating lords of parliament by *patent*, and this further consolidated the membership of the Lords in the hands of the Crown. This is the process now employed in making a peer.

In this way arose the peers as distinct from the other nobles—and it will be observed from what has just been said that they were not

---

[1] Grand sergeantry is when a manor or other feu is held by a nominal rent, such as the delivery of a trout, as in one case in Cornwall, or a rose, as for Dunstaffnage Castle, as rental to the Superior.

necessarily derived from the older or greater barons of the realm. Peerage, as such, is not some species of higher, *uradel*. Among the peers there were, and are, some in this category—but there are as many or more outside of it.

A point which has to be stressed is that all the nobles who possessed baronies or manors, whether held *in capite* or of other barons were

Arms of Docwra

barons or lords. All were styled in Latin, for instance, *dominus*. This fact is still evident from the use of the term lord, for the holder of a manor, in *lord of the manor*. In Scotland we get the same term, in the Scottish form of *laird*, for the lord of a barony, and other principal nobles, such as chiefs. However, in England, since the lords of parliament continued to be styled barons, although all lords of manors were also barons, this title has come to be limited to *lords of parliament*, usually called *Lords*. However, the term baron itself just meant *man*, a baron being his superior's man.[1] An echo of this is to be found in the motto of the Lords (Grand Priors) of St. John in the Middle Ages, whose motto was originally *Sans Baro* (later corrupted to *Sane Baro*). Its precise meaning is not clear, but it has been thought that these Lords considered themselves Barons without superior.   The figure on page 127 shows the arms of the sixteenth century Prior Docwra with his motto of *Sans Baro*. It also appears upon his standard, and it will be found on the arms of the last Grand Prior of England, temp. Henry VIII, Sir William Werton, K. M.   The use of this motto till as late as the sixteenth century suggests that the meaning of the word baron was still current knowledge, at least among the learned, as referring to all fee-holding lords.

In these days it cannot be too frequently stressed (in the English-speaking countries where there is not merely widespread ignorance of the facts, but an unfortunate use of the word *noble* for *peer* which only serves to create confusion) that peerage is a dignity but it is not an organic order of society. It never has been anywhere in Christian feudal Europe.   In fact there has been in some countries, such as Poland,[2] to quote an instance, considerable resistance to the creation of peerage, and when created, to its extension, especially among the older and more powerful nobles, on the grounds that peerage is an extension of the powers of the state over the nobles, the natural leaders of the people.   Peerage as it operates today in Britain probably has some of these undesirable characteristics, as titles are not conferred upon people who are natural leaders of organic communities within the realms concerned, but for primarily political and economic reasons, some of which, in terms of nobiliary law, do not justify the conferment of the peerage at all !

This difference between the peers, or greater barons or nobles, and the lesser barons and nobles led to the two-fold classification of the nobility into *nobiles majores* and *nobiles minores*.   It is a wholly wrong use of the term noble, therefore, to restrict it to the peerage, just as it is to use the term baron for lord—since all lords of manors, and all feudal barons in Scotland, are all as much barons as any lord of

---

[1] A. R. Wagner, *English Genealogy*, Oxford, 1960, p. 89.
[2] L. G. Pine, *Heraldry and Genealogy*. The English Universities Press Ltd., London, 1957.

parliament.   In this latter case, unfortunately, it is official classification in England to call lords barons.[1]

One important result of this confused use of the term baron and noble for Lord Barons of parliament and Peers respectively in England has been that foreigners have concluded that there are very few nobles in England !   Thus, in the early part of the nineteenth century it was said that there were 580,000 nobles in Russia, 239,000 in Austria, and in Spain, in 1785, 479,000 nobles, and in France at the Revolution 365,000 noble families, whereas, in Great Britain there were only 300 ! Actually there were in 1798 9,458 armigerous, that is noble, families in England and 4,000 in Scotland.[2]   Even as late as 1958, at the *International Congress for Heraldry and Genealogy*, there were certain French members of the congress who (accepting the English term noble at its face value) considered that there were only as many nobles as there were peers of the realm !

It might be observed here that while from the mid sixteenth century the term *Noble* in England tends to become, wrongly, more and more restricted to peers, and by the end of that century is often so confusingly used in Scotland also, earlier documents, and some contemporary ones, use it in its proper sense.   For instance, we find in Rymer that in 1283 the ravages by the Welsh are referred to as *strages magnatum, nobilium et aliorum*—the destruction of lords, nobles, and others.   Here nobles means the noblesse apart from the peers.   In the Register of Ely[3] we read of a meeting in 1458, where it says " Peyton and Thomas Lockton, Esquires, *and many other nobles (aliis nobilibus)* ".   Perkin Warbeck, temp. Henry VII, in his proclamation, accuses the King by saying he caused divers nobles to be killed, and then cites them by name not one of whom was a peer.   In Doncaster Church[4] there was an inscription of a squire who died in 1465 in which he is described as

---

[1] But there is no reason why so confusing a term should be used in Scotland, where we still employ the term baron in its ancient sense for the feudal baronage, and where (with chiefs) we call them lairds or lords.   That is why apart from using *Lord* in front of the name to make it clear the person is a peer, the only other sensible way of doing so in order to prevent confusion is to call him a *peer* or *lord of parliament*.

[2] Sir James Lawrence, Knight of Malta, on the *Nobility of British Gentry*, Paris, 1828, p. 2.

[3] Harl. MS. 5828.

[4] Harl. MS. 801.

Noble. Again, Clarenceux's letters patent to Nicholas Mattock, in the ninth year of Henry VII (1494),[1] talks of gentle and noble men, in that order, meaning by the latter term not *peers*, but all the *noblesse*. Dugdale gives an account in connection with Henry VIII's summons to Parliament in his 21st year (1560), which states that His Grace was accompanied by " the substance of the Noblemen of this his realm— The procession began with the Noblemen as Knights and Esquires according to their degree, then the judges, the bishops, then the arch- bishop and the chancellor Sir Thomas Moore, then the officers of

Camden

state preceded the King, who was followed by the Temporal lords according to their estates and ancienties ".

The same meaning is quite clearly given to the interpretation of noble by Camden, Claren- ceux King of Arms, who died in 1623, in his *Britannia—nobilies minores sunt equites aurati, armigeri et qui vulgo generosi, et gentle men vocantur.* (The minor nobility are knights, esquires and those who are called generosi or gentlemen.)

Indeed, throughout Camden's letters patent we find this use of the term noble for all armigerous persons, and not peers alone. In the fifth book of *The Boke of St. Albans* (p. 4) a clear statement is given that the French divided, at that time, the sixteenth century, their populace into *les nobles et la populare, ou gentilshomes et villains*, while the English divided theirs into four classes of (I) gentlemen, (II) citizens, (III) yeomen, and (IV) artificers and labourers. It goes on to say that knights, esquires and gentlemen are *nobilitas minor—for they in parliament have no place among the Lords*. Here we have a clear use of the term noble, as in many other places in the same work, for all the noblesse— that is the whole armigerous population which was above citizen, yeoman, mechanic and labourer.

Sir James Lawrence, K.M., cites Peacham's *Compleat Gentleman* (1634) where we read that Coats of Arms are " Shuffled into records and monuments by painters, glaziers, carvers, and such ; but so good

[1] Harl. MS. 1507, B.M.

an order has been lately established by the Earl Marshal, that this sinister dealing is cut off from such mercenary abuses of nobility ". He also draws attention to *Whittaker's Richmondshire* where there is recorded an inscription of 1664 at Romaldkirk, in which a knight is called The Most Noble Lord Francis Apelby of Lartington. (Nobilissimus Dominus Franciscus Apelby de Lartington.) He likewise quotes Jacob's Law Dictionary where it says that Clarenceux's duty is to marshall the funerals of " all the lesser *nobility*, knights or esquires, south of Trent ", peers being Garter's prerogative.[1]

Lord Lyon Sir Alex. Erskine (appointed 1677) also talks of " the arms of Peers, prelates, barons, and other nobles of this Kingdom ".[2] We will also find in the matriculations of Orrock of that ilk (Vol. I, p. 529 of *The Public Register of All Arms and Bearings in Scotland*), and Mackenzie of Hiltoun (Vol. I, p. 374) that these persons are described as noble.[3]

In the following passage the eighteenth century English herald, Edmondson, makes clear that despite the English use of the word Noble for Peer, which had become well-established by that time, a *gentleman* was a noble : He says—

" Accordingly, ever since the decline of the Roman Empire, the word *nobilis* hath generally been used as well for one who is by the Emperor's Letters Patent, Codicilli honorarii, or otherwise raised to the rank here spoken of, as he who is so by birth ; and in this sense also *nobilis* hath since been used in England, but yet totally distinct from our other notion of *Noble*, which we use when we express our Lords and Peers by the *Noblemen*. Among the Danes, Swedes, and other their Northern neighbours, the Latin *Nobilis* is denoted by Adel or Edel ; as they call Gentlemen . . . More might be adduced to elucidate the subject ; what hath been already offered sufficiently shews that Adel, Edel, Nobilis, and Gentlemen, have one and the same signification ; that the title of Gentleman was very anciently in high esteem ; and that the rank and degree of the Ordo Equestris of the Sacred Roman Empire, *die freye vom Adel, die freye Adeliche Reichs Ritterscheft, the free Gentlemen of the Empire*, or however the persons composing that body may be otherwise styled is truly honourable, respectable, and noble ".[4]

---

[1] *Op. cit.*, pp. 34 and 35.
[2] Innes of Learney, *Diploma of Nobility for De Landa*. *The Juridical Review*, Vol. LII, No. 3, Sept. 1940, p. 194.
[3] *Ut supra*, p. 190.
[4] Joseph Edmondson, *A Complete Body of Heraldry*, London, 1780, Vol. I, p. 2 of the section " Ordo Equestris of the Roman Empire."

K

Sufficient has been given to establish the meaning of nobility as comprehending the whole of the *noblesse*, and no heraldic work can use the term in any other way, except at the expense of being inconsistent with past usage and being unintelligible to foreign readers who still use the term in the correct manner. While the usage of nobility for peerage began in Tudor times it did not become absolute in the customary use of England till Dr. Samuel Johnson defined a gentleman as not noble. But he was no authority in such matters and the time has come to restore to the word its real meaning.

Sir James Lawrence suggests that the use of the term *Nobles* for *Peers* arose because many peers were not (as is still the case) *gentry*, and so could not be called gentlemen[1] (the significance of which we shall shortly discuss) but could be called nobles, as they had become members of the nobility in right of both their peerage and their arms. Consequently a word which we shall show was lower in connotation throughout Europe than gentleman came to be given an inverted importance in England, whence it spread to Ireland and Scotland—although in the latter country this common meaning has somewhat been held in check by the heraldic authority's continued use of *noble* for all armigers.

Within the nobility of the feudal period what was at first considered much more important than *peerage rank*, and to the end retained its estimation, was *gentility*. Gentility had much the significance which attached to the Roman *gens* from which the word is derived. The *gentes* were ancient noble clan communities of Rome which had existed from early times, and had not acquired their nobility in later times, by purchase, ennoblement or any other means.[2]

Thus, as Sir James Lawrence, K.M.,[3] in his little book on the subject made quite clear, gentility is superior to nobility, since gentility is inherited from the past, it is innate, whereas nobility may be

---

[1] Sir James Lawrence, Knight of Malta, *On the Nobility of British Gentry*, Paris, 1828, p. 83.

[2] Mr. Hankinson, Editor of *Debrett's Peerage*, 1957 edition, p. 183, draws attention to the view that the word gentleman was derived from one of two companies of particularly distinguished soldiers, mostly of good families, towards the end of the Roman Empire, who were called *Gentiles*. The other were the *Scutarii*. It has been suggested that the titles *gentleman* and *esquire* derive from these.

[3] Sir James Lawrence, Knight of Malta, *op. cit.*, p. 2.

acquired. " Noblemen may be only persons of rank and distinction ; but gentlemen must be persons of family and quality—*Fit nobilis, nascitur generosus* "—a nobleman is made, a gentleman is born.

The word noble, comes from *nobilis*, the original and basic meaning of which is *known*. The feudal conquerors of Europe were recognised, accepted, or known to their princely leaders—and so nobles. When heraldry became an operative system of distinguishing men in Europe, owners of arms were *known* by their arms, and so the arms became the tokens of nobility, for without the arms the nobles would not be known. In the all-encasing armour there was no other efficient way of being known except by the arms. Consequently, without arms there could be no state of being known and recognised, and taken account of, by one's peers and superiors. But once patents of nobility and grants of arms were made by the Sovereign, and later, as we have seen in Scotland, by the King of Arms with the implicit conferment of nobility in the grant of arms, there was no way to distinguish in this mass of the *known* between the *ancient* and *new men*.

It was at this stage that the term *gentle*,[1] carrying with it the connotation of *gens*, the state of being descended from an ancient tribal or clan group of nobles, came to have a very special significance, and became the distinguishing factor between the ancient aristocracy and the new. We get the use of it for the old aristocracy in the following passage concerning the aftermath of the disastrous battle of Tewkesbury when Edward IV of England won a bloody victory—

> " This batayll thus done and atchived, and kyngs grace thus largely shewed, it was so that, in the abbey and othar places of the towne, were founden Edmond, callyd Duke of Somerset, the prior of Seynt Johns, called Ser John Longestrother, Ser Thomas Tressham, Ser Gervaux of Clyfton, knyghts, squiers, and other notable parsonnes dyvers, whiche all, dyvers tymes, were browght afore the Kyng's brothar, the Duke of Gloucester and Constable of England, and the Duke of Norfolke, Marshall of England, theyr judges ; and so were judged to deathe, in the mydst of the towne, Edmond Duke of

---

[1] Derived from *gentrice*, from the old French *geneterise* for *gentelise*, equivalent to the Latin *generosus*, derived from *gentilis*, meaning a person of a *race* or gens ; from which *gentleman* is equivalent to the French *gentlehomme*, meaning a nobleman of ancestry, and found in Italian as *gentiluomo*.

Somerset, and the sayd Prior of Seint Johns, *with many other gentils* that there were taken ".[1]

A gentleman was *born* of ancient ancestry and while a noble might be a gentleman it is true, he might equally be only a newly created noble. For this reason, it should be pointed out in passing, that it is hardly proper in British patents of arms for the grantee to be styled a gentleman, for a King of Arms has not the power to make a gentleman. Mackenzie of Rosehaugh[2] says—" But yet the Prince may still bestow Arms, without restriction, though he cannot properly make a Gentleman : for that comes by Blood, and not by Patent ". It is for this reason that we find King James VI and I saying to his nurse, in answer to her importunities on behalf of her son, that he could make him a peer but not a gentleman. For the same reason, as Sir James Lawrence, K.M., has pointed out[3]—" Bonaparte, in the plenitude of his power, though he created dukes and grand-dukes and kings, never ventured to make a gentleman. Only persons of ancient noblesse are there styled gentlemen ". The significance of gentleman is seen when the Lord Lyon adjudicates on the arms of a *chief of a family of name* when the arms are invariably referred to a *tesserae gentilitatis*[4] and not *nobilitatis*.[5]

This distinction between *noble* and *gentle* is observed also in other countries as well as our own. For instance in Portugal we have *noble* and *fidalgo*, the latter being the same as our *gentleman*.

It is obvious that if *gentleman* meant a man of *ancient* nobility, some means had to be adopted in order to evaluate it. There thus grew up the " proofs of nobility " as they are called. These varied from country to country, and from one corporation of knights to another.

In Germany the only proof accepted normally was that of 16 quarterings. This was also imposed in the Church in Germany, and

---

[1] *Histories of the Arrivall of Edward IV in England* and the Finall Recouerye of his Kingdomes from Henry VI. A.D. MCCCCLXXI, Camden Socy., MDCCCXXXVIII.

[2] *The Science of Heraldry*, Edinburgh, 1680, p. 12.

[3] *Op cit.*, p. 124.

[4] Or according to the ancient heraldic writer Silvester Petra Sancta *Tesserae Gentilitiae*, tickets or *warrants of gentility*.

[5] Sir Thomas Innes of Learney (Frank Adam's) *Clans, Septs, and Regiments of the Scottish Highlands*, Edinburgh, 1955, p. 196 and at other places.

it was often impossible for a man to obtain a canonry, or to hold any medium to high office in the ruling branches of the Church in Germany (and elsewhere too) without being able to advance his proofs of nobility. Sixteen quarterings meant that all his great great grandparents without exception had to be noble, and the proof of this nobility was the production not only of the names and styles of each of these families, but their arms as well. In other countries the proofs were not always so strict, and they were in Italy, and in Britain, for instance, normally four quarters—that is all the grandparents had to be noble and armigerous. However, there were cases in Germany, in particular, where as many as 32 quarterings were demanded.

Such proofs were demanded by all the great orders of knighthood, such as of St. John, of Rhodes and Malta, of the Temple, and of the Teutonic Order, the Garter, the Golden Fleece, Thistle, and the like, while it was impossible for a man to take part in a tournament, which nearly every young nobleman, who was seeking to advance his way at court, had to do, without advancing his proofs of nobility. The Laws of Arms, that is of the Courts Martial, which governed the rules of the tournaments make this clear—and go further, by ordering that if anyone tried to participate in them with deficient nobility he was to be branded as infamous.

In Britain, and particularly England, there was a tendency from an early period to replace these proofs by one based solely on the male descent—and in these cases long linear descent (which is the normal one still maintained by British families) of anything up to five centuries was demanded. This type of proof is still demanded of the British aspirants to become of *Honour and Devotion* in the Knighthood of Malta, and has recently been permitted to Hungarians as well, the nobility of family having to go back to before 1485.[1]

It will be seen that these were the defences which the older class of feudal nobles, descended from the conquering Gothonic and German warriors, erected in an attempt to protect themselves from the intrusions of new men among them. By these means they hoped to keep them in their place, and at a distance, until such time, with

[1] R. Gayre of Gayre and Nigg, *The Heraldry of the Knights of St. John*, Allahabad, 1956, p. 116.

gathering antiquity, the new men qualified to be reckoned as gentry also. We might also say they were an indirect resistance to the powers of the Sovereign—or the state.

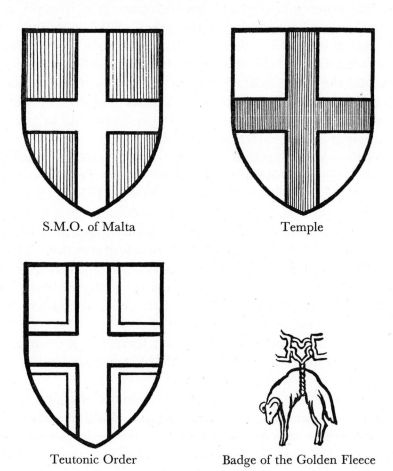

S.M.O. of Malta

Temple

Teutonic Order

Badge of the Golden Fleece

We shall see shortly from a quotation by Mackenzie of Rosehaugh from the distinguished English herald Camden that the granting of arms made a gentleman of coat armour, and that it took three generations before gentry of blood was achieved. This was evidently the English law on the matter, and in that case it was no different from that of Scotland or other countries where the proof of nobility of four armigerous grandparents was accepted as the proof to distinguish a gentleman from a noble. We get a reflection of this idea in the regulations made by James VI and I for the founding of the order of baronets. In it he instructed the commissioners charged with the examination of the qualifications of candidates, that—" provided always, that you proceed with none, except it shall appear unto you upon good proof, that they are men for quality, state of living, and good reputation worthy of the same : *and that they are at least descended of a Grandfather* by the Father's side that bare Armes ".

We may add that the assumption here is that it is only necessary to prove the three generations on the male side, simply because the ennobled, once he was a noble, that is a gentleman of coat armour, would see to it that his sons married gentlewomen, and also his grandsons. There is no doubt that this led in time to the idea that it was unnecessary to prove any other descent than that of the pronominal line, till today, that is the only proof of descent now normally offered in British heraldic practice.[1]

The very real meaning that attached to gentleman, and does still in nobiliary law, as something acquired by time, led to the conception that gentility started in the grantee, grew in his son, and reached fruition in his grandson. This rule of distinguishing between the generation in which the nobility was conferred and that in which it was accepted as noble by birth, existed because, as Edmondson[2] informs us, the *jus nobilitatis* (nobiliary law) was founded on the Roman law of the *jus imaginum*. The erecting of family statues had the same significance in Rome as arms had in feudalism. He who was not permitted to erect a statue was an *ignobilis*. The man who was allowed to erect one was *novus* (which equated with the ennobled generation) and he who inherited statues was a *nobilis*.

In armory there is a curious misuse of the term gentleman, for instead of classifying the grantee as a noble—perhaps because since late Tudor times the whole terminology has been bedevilled by the wrongful use of noble for peer—he has come to be called a *gentleman of*

---

[1] Until the 20th century, when it has become a commonplace for peers and gentlemen to marry barmaids, chorus girls, and the like, no other proof was really necessary as the number who married out of their caste, once they had achieved admission to it, was small.

[2] Joseph Edmondson, *A Complete Body of Heraldry*, London, 1780, Vol. I, p. 8.

coat armour. Thus, the *Boke of St. Albans* says, under the heading of he who is a *gentleman of coat armour and not of blood*, that he is a gentleman whose device (arms) is " by an herald igouen ", or, he is a yeoman who, having received a patent of a lordship from the King, may wear the " cotarmour of the same lordshyp ", and so on.[1] While Sir George Mackenzie of Rosehaugh[2] remarks—" And Camden informs us, That of old there was a distinction betwixt Gentleman of Blood, and Gentleman of Coat-armour ; and that the third from him who first had Coat-armour, was to all effects and purposes a Gentleman of Blood, pag. 157.2." [3]

There is no doubt that it was from this use of the word gentleman that the heralds have come to concede it to a grantee, in the sense that he is a *gentleman* of *coat armour*. But as we have shown, neither they, nor the Queen, can make a gentleman of any sort, as only history makes gentry.[4] For the sake of exact and legal use of terms it would be better for the Kings of Arms to use the proper style of *nobleman* instead of gentleman in the patents of grantees.

A second misuse of the term gentleman flowed from these premises. For if a grantee became a gentleman of coat armour, then he was a species of gentleman, and if so, anyone holding the style of a noble in the realm, (which such a grantee was) was carrying the *port of a gentleman*, whether he was in fact a gentleman or a noble only or neither. From this flows the common customary misuse of the term in English in England. Everyone of education, every west-end club member, every product of an English public school, considers he is *per se*, a

---

[1] A yeoman, according to *The Boke of St. Albans*, could also take the arms of a gentleman he had slain in battle, and, by that act he ennobled himself. It should be remembered that there was not a great gulf between the yeomanry and nobility, since their orders were both derived from the original free conquerors of many countries.

[2] The *Science of Heraldry*, Edinburgh, 1680, p. 12.

[3] In addition to the proof of *perfect blood* in Britain, which was that of these three generations, there was the further one of *ancestry* which Hugh Clark mentions in the following terms— " To make perfection in blood, a lineal descent from *Atavus, Proavus, Avus, Pater* (the great-grandfather's father, the great-grandfather, the grandfather, and the father), on the father's side, was required ; and as much on the mother's side ; then was a gentleman not only of perfect blood, but of ancestry also ". *An Introduction to Heraldry*, 1859, p. 242.

[4] Selden, *Table-Talk*, goes so far as to say that even the Almighty cannot make a gentleman !

gentleman. He believes he has a *right* to be called a gentleman. He repudiates with indignation any suggestion to the contrary. But, for all that if he does not establish it by assize of arms [1] he is not *legally* to be received *of proven right* as a gentleman before any court of honour, nor in any international order of knighthood, nor among legitimist nobility on the Continent, although his style of living may well be that which we associate with the gentry.

How significant is the term gentleman will be seen when we remember that George IV considered it the highest flattery to be called the First Gentleman of Europe ; and, King Umberto II, despite all his titles, prefers to be styled First Gentleman of Italy. While in France, under the old regime, it was ruled a gentleman could walk beside Dukes, who were the peers,[2] and only gentlemen (as *gentlemen*) had the right to step into the King's carriage and be received by him at royal hunts—while numerous peers, who were not gentlemen, were denied this right.[3]

George IV

It may be pointed out that while the ancient nobility's insistence on its rights in such matters as this have been interpreted as some form of anti-social opposition to human progress and advancement, it is very doubtful if such a view can be sustained. The greatest menace to man's liberty, in the end, comes from an all-pervading and dominant

---

[1] Or otherwise before a Court of Chivalry.

[2] Men of title of lower rank were not, in France, as they are with us, peers.

[3] While, even more disastrous to peerage pretensions, in the reign of Louis XVI an ordinance appeared that no one should be presented at Versailles, unless he could prove 400 years of gentility, or that his ancestors were already noble before the year 1400. As a consequence of this, " a multiplicity of comtes and marquises were rejected ; though many an untitled gentleman, ancient as our squires in their halls in Lancashire and Northumberland, left their towers and chateaux in Brittany and Languedoc, and posted up to Paris to show their pre-eminence. Every gentleman, his pedigree being certified, was, on the first hunting-day, invited to mount with the king into his carriage, and accompany His Majesty to the spot where the hounds were turned out. This privilege was termed *le droit de monter dans le carosse du roi*. The plain squire, to whom this right was allowed, was considered as superior to the count or marquis, whose claims were rejected ". Sir James Lawrence, K.M., *On the Nobility of the British Gentry, op. cit.*, pp. 97-98

State against which individuals or even orders of society cannot make any successful resistance. For if the State can create every kind of privilege, political, legal and social, then there is an end of liberty, since all must conform to the ruling cliques in the political system on whose advice the Crown is bound to act. It is right that there should be certain areas of human organisation which should be outside the combined power of money and political privilege and which can, to that extent, serve to redress the balance. If there is a class in the nation which considers that its status is not necessarily enhanced by some decorations conferred in what one comedian has recently referred to as " the annual prize-givings ", it means there are, to that extent, that number of persons not susceptible to the dangers of corruption by the bribery which a massive wielding of such patronage by the head of the ruling party of the day exercises.

Further confusion has been produced in Britain by a lack of appreciation of the significance of the term *esquire*.[1] In all the precedency tables esquire is put before gentleman, and so many fall into the fault of thinking that esquires are of older or more important families than gentlemen. Here again, as we have seen between peer and noble, we have the confusion between an organic order of society and a mere rank. All the aristocracy are nobles, of whom the most considerable in the estimation of nobiliary law in the past, and still we venture to think internationally regarded, are the gentry. The peers are a rank in the nobility and while members of the peerage may be gentry, many of them may not yet qualify for the designation of gentlemen at all, as both their peerage and nobility may be of quite recent extraction. We can, therefore, have the curious situation that a man may be an Earl but not a gentleman, and could be so branded without fear of being accused of slandering him. In the same way knight and esquire are two further ranks, which arose directly out of war, and the furnishing of the armies with officers in the form of knights and their lieutenants, or probationers, who were esquires.

From this there came about the creation of esquires to princes from the nobility, and, finally, certain offices were considered to be

---

[1] Esquires existed before the reign of Richard II, but it was not until then that it was used as a title. J. Cussans, *Handbook of Heraldry*, London, 1882, p. 214.

esquiral in rank.   Lords of manors sometimes subscribed themselves as esquires, but more often than not preferred, if they were of ancient families, to call themselves gentlemen.   Anyone holding a feu which is considered sufficient to establish a territorial house in the realm is entitled to the rank of esquire—if he wants it.   He can actually be at the same time both an esquire in precedency and a gentleman in the order of his nobility.   The only person who cannot be both is he who is either of new hereditary nobility, or the man who is personally noble only by reason of holding an office, which is reckoned as of esquiral degree for purposes of precedency, such as being a mayor or provost, holder of the Queen's commission in the rank of captain and above in the Army, and so on.   Chiefs of names, and their heirs apparent, are hereditary esquires as well as gentlemen.[1]   Since the fifteenth century the dignity of esquire (as well as gentleman) has, in Scotland, had to be determined in courts of chivalry according to the Law of Arms, just as it was in the English Court of Chivalry also.[2]

However, owing to this failure to realise that gentleman means a man of *ancient* and *proven* nobility, whereas esquire is purely a rank, which anyone can hold, whether he is noble by birth or not, there has developed in England the idea that gentleman is the lowest form of noble.   But this is clearly nothing of the kind.   In any gathering of nobles from many countries, where the rules of British precedency could not be applied, there is little doubt that precedency would have to rest on the main considerations of international nobiliary law, and gentry would certainly rank before esquires as such, and could, probably, before knighthood as such, and before all peerage which was not yet gentry, just as they did in France, in the instance we have quoted under *le droit de monter dans le carosse du roi*.

It should be observed in passing that the word *quality*, used so frequently in older English books means *gentry*.   In that use it is still found in some of the formal patents of the heralds.   They were usually given the designations of *your worship*, and *your honour*, which titles have

---

[1] Sir Aeneas Macpherson, Advocate, in *Loyall Dissuasive*.

[2] Also in France, under the old code, the title of *ecuyer* was the subject of legislation.   A fine of 500 louis d'or was levied in favour of the nearest hospital for its improper use.   T. Innes of Learney, *Diploma of Nobility for De Landa*, The Juridical Rev., Vol. LII, No. 3, Sept. 1940, p. 197.

only survived in general use in England where those holding noble offices, such as of mayor and justices of the peace, are concerned. They were also styled *honourable*. The restriction of this style to the children of peers is a relatively recent innovation, for it rightly belongs to all gentry.[1] It was, and is, the English language equivalent of *Nobile* as a prefix in Italy, or *Noble* in Malta. Thus in Malta a noble is addressed as The Noble, to distinguish him from a baron who is *The Most Noble*.

There is another fact which should be remembered when considering the position of the gentry *vis à vis* the peerage. It is, as we have already pointed out elsewhere, that no peer was permitted, when the Laws of Arms were still able to control jousting and tournament, under which the law of the duel came, to refuse the challenge of a gentleman.[2]

Thus, in the fourth book of *The Boke of St. Albans*, p. 57, we read

> A Gentleman well borne and descended from Parentage of foure degrees, may fight with any Earle or Baron, in case of Treason to his Prince or Countrie, and also murther and infidelitie, because they are (besides their dignitie) none other than Gentlemen, and Gentilite or Nobilitie is hereditarie and cannot bee taken away, but Dignitie may.

John Selden in *The Duello or Single Combat*, published at London 1610 (p. 10), tells us much the same thing, namely that four quarters

---

[1] The styles were given to these two classes (magistrates and peers' children) because in the main they were originally gentry and so entitled to them, and what we have seen, as Sir James Lawrence has pointed out, is the leaving off of those styles by the gentry once peers and magistrates began to be created from people whom they considered of lesser nobiliary rank than themselves, and they tended to accept only the style of Your Honour—which, incidentally, still lingers on in Ireland and in India. *On the Nobility of the British Gentry*, Paris, 1828, p. 64.

[2] Mackenzie of Rosehaugh. *Observations upon the Laws and Customs of Nations as to Precedency*, Edinburgh, 1680, p. 31. " Nobility is devided with Us, as in England in *Nobiles Majores* and *Minores*, the Greater and the Lesser Nobility : Under the Greater are comprehended all such as are Lords of Parliament : Under the Lesser are comprehended Knights and Gentlemen. And though all these be not Peers of Parliament, yet they are all Peers to one another ; And thus a Gentleman may be offered to a Dukes Daughter, whose Ward and Marriage falls to the King, as has been often decyded, nor can that Match be refused upon the account of Inequality : And it hath been found, that though Noblemen [Peers] must be judged by their Peers, yet Landed Gentlemen may pass upon their Assyse ; and a Nobleman [Peer] is obliged to accept of a Challenge from a Gentleman as his Peer, where Duels are lawful ".

of gentility were necessary to undertake the duel or tournament, in these words—

> Henry of Germany surnamed the Fouler . . . was in his owne territories author hereof, annexing certain lawes, among which one was thus, That hee, which was not of generous stocke, *deg. sua nobilitate quatuor auorum natalibus docere non poterit*, (being, not able to show his own nobility by 4 grandparents) should by no meanes bee admitted as a party in the Launce-controversies.

Here we have the condition clearly stated, and it is generous stock of four generations (that is full gentility of race) and not peerage dignity that was required in the combatant.

On the other hand while a peer could not refuse a gentleman in a duel he could a plebeian, and even a newly created noble—or at least there is some doubt as to where the latter stood in this respect.

Selden

In the same way (as we have already observed elsewhere) even in the Middle Ages a simple gentleman could make a match with any peer's daughter. Such a marriage was not a misalliance. This Sir John Ferne writing in 1586 makes clear—

> If a duchess, countess, or baroness, marry with but a simple gentleman, she loseth her dignity ; we say the reason is this *Quando foemina nobilis nupserit ignobili, desinit esse nobilis* (when a noble female marries a plebeian she ceases to be noble) ; *but in so doing we misquote the text, which means if any gentlewoman, which in our laws is called nobilis, do marry a man of no coat armour (whom also we call ignobilem), her state and title of gentleness is in suspense.* (Our italics.)

He goes on to say that in the reign of Mary Tudor two cases were raised by the lawyers whether widows of peers, having married gentlemen, might retain their titles, quoting *Quando foemina* etc. as above. The heralds categorically stated the law was misquoted. They lost their titles, not because their husbands were not noble, *since they were registered as such*, but because a woman must take her rank from her husband.

We have seen that the nobility of Europe arose in the main out of a conquering caste, and it held by military tenure. Consequently, it

followed that it did all the fighting, and the gentry everywhere provided the officers, and the yeomanry mainly foot soldiery. The
peasant was in most realms excused from military service. In place
of it he paid taxes in one form or another, from which the aristocracy
were exempt.[1]   It followed, therefore, that on the passing of the Middle
Ages, and the creation of national standing armies, which needed
officers, the same class was called upon for military service. Consequently, throughout Europe, until two centuries ago nearly all
officers were in fact gentlemen of blood. Much of the chivalry which
remained in war, and which has been progressively eliminated since
the French Revolutionary wars, and which is banished altogether
under the impact of the last two world wars, was due to this
fact. Thus an officer could give his parole, as he had been able
to do as a knight or esquire when taken prisoner in the Middle Ages.
His captors not only hoped that he would keep it but they knew that
as a gentleman he would in fact do so. Officers could still lead their
men, and wear different and more splendid uniforms, because up to
the French Revolution, when the bitter total annihilating type of
nationalistic war was created, no conscious attempt was made to
wipe out the officers as a class, and the only added danger which they
ran was that which was attendant upon the fact that they led their
men. It was because of this that Wellington took no precautions when
riding his outpost as in the Peninsular War, only to be shot at by a
French sniper ! Here again, we see the chivalry arising out of a noble
society : for Wellington bowed to the Frenchman, and the latter,
despite his revolutionary fervour, felt deep down in himself ashamed of
what he had done, and so he stood to attention and presented arms !

[1] This was the reason why nobles of one country found it necessary to be admitted as
nobles of another. Thus we find down to the French Revolution, Scottish gentlemen, for
instance, producing from Lyon evidence of their nobility to the French authorities. An example
of this, quoted by Sir James Lawrence, *op. cit.*, pp. 91-2, from the nobiliaire of Brittany—
" Ledit André Scot obtint . . . lettres-patentes datées d'Edimburg du II novembre 1669, par
esquelles ce Prince [Charles II] le déclara noble et issu du neuvième degré de Michel Scot,
baron de Balneri, chevalier doré, ambassadeur en Norwège, l'an 1285. Ces lettres furent
confirmées par autres lettres-patentes du feu roi Louis XIV du 7 mars 1671, enregistrées au
parlement de Rennes le 20 desdits mois et an ; e c'est en faveur de ces lettres que le même
André fut maintenu dans la possession de sa noblesse, par arrêt des commissaires de la Bretagne,
etc. Armes, d'or à trois têtes de lion de gueules, arraches et langues d'azur ".

In our day we would have given a decoration and promotion to anyone who had killed Rommel in North Africa. Thus, as we have passed away from the noble structure of society so have our standards of chivalry fallen.[1]

This fact that officers had to be gentlemen had an important result following the French Revolution, and the various democratisations of certain European countries.[2] Logically most continental armies struck the word *gentleman* out of military law, as officers had no longer to be of the gentry. But in Britain, illogically, the law was retained, so far as the designation of the officer is concerned, but it was ignored so far as the appointments go ! Therefore, while the army and other services are open to anyone irrespective of birth, all officers are still called *gentlemen* : and we get the actual indictment in military law, of " conduct unbecoming an officer and a gentleman ". Since most of them are not gentlemen especially in the wartime armies, it is quite unfair that they should be tried for not behaving as gentlemen should !

As Sir James Lawrence, K.M. [3] has pointed out, the same rule held good as to the law, and, in England, only a gentleman could be admitted to the Inns of Court, and hence the coats of arms which decorate the halls of such places as the Temple and Lincoln's Inn.

[1] Lord Winterton, speaking on the wireless, on 19th April, 1959, described how even as late as the 1914-18 war, the former Austrian Ambassador to the Court of St. James used to arrange for British officer prisoners of war to be allowed out of prison on parole to attend the races as his guests ! It is significant that this chivalry to an enemy in misfortune was extended, not by the brash German state, but by the ancient, highly aristocratic and legitimist Austrian. Those held prisoner by the Austrians considered themselves highly fortunate compared with those held by the Germans.

Such survival of ancient good manners and humane feeling was not entirely one-sided. I remember my friend the late Herr Oswald Arning, of Hamburg, telling me that in 1914, on returning from South Africa to Germany to fight for the Kaiser, his ship ran into a British fleet, and he was taken prisoner and placed on board a troopship carrying his English uncle's cavalry regiment, into whose keeping he was placed on parole. He landed with the regiment, lived with it all the time it was training in England, riding with the officers, until the day they embarked for France when he was handed over by his uncle to the prison authorities !

[2] We are, of course, referring to direct commissioning as officers. Even before the French Revolution officers could rise from the ranks, and we have pointed out elsewhere that three generations of regular army commissioned service, could, in such cases, bestow nobility on the family.

[3] *Op. cit.*, p. 116. Also Hugh Clark, *An Introduction to Heraldry*, 1859, pp. 242-3—" anciently, none were admitted into the Inns of Court but such as were gentlemen of blood ".

The same thing is true of magistrates, since those who held the Prince's commission of peace in olden times could only be gentry. Had they not been they would not have been able to exercise it as the gentry would hardly have been likely to accept the jurisdiction of an inferior member of society over their order.   In this way, magistrates became recognised as in rank higher than gentry, and so esquires, while they have retained the style of gentry by being addressed as " your honour " and " your worship ".

We have written at length on this subject in order to put these titles of noble, peer, gentleman and esquire in their proper legal perspectives.[1]

There is another consideration which should be borne in mind when we are evaluating the relative status of gentility and peerage, and that is the situation which arises when a cadet of a gentle family is of higher rank in the English or Scottish Precedency Tables than the Chief of his Name.   This is a particularly important question even to the present time in Scotland, both because tribo-feudality is still a living reality, and because this reality finds its expression in gatherings of clans and families, as well as in the active application of brisures to all cadet arms.

Sir James Lawrence [2] as well as the present Lord Lyon in many of his writings, has drawn attention to the fact that a peer is not necessarily the head of his house—but may well be a younger branch.   As a consequence, in such a case, his arms bear a brisure, and he is in respect of his paternal arms inferior to his chief who is untitled, or of a lesser peerage rank.   He is superior in the hierarchy of peerage to his familial chief, but he is equally subordinate by the law of family, clan

---

[1] We are, of course, well aware that the two latter titles with that of lady, are also abused in quite another way by the masses.   Every man is addressed as esquire and every public convenience has to be labelled for *Ladies* and for *Gentlemen*, and no one can be referred to (particularly in England) without one or the other honorific being bestowed.   The custom is so strong that it was already established even a century or more ago, for Sir James Lawrence, K.M., points out that at that time even the " King of England addresses the Two Houses of Parliament, 'My lords and gentlemen'.   The members address their constituents, and the promiscuous rabble at the hustings, Gentlemen !   The rabble return to their pothouses, and address each other, Gentlemen !   The word gentlemen re-echoes from one end of the kingdom to the other ".   *Op. cit.*, p. 121.

[2] *Ut supra*, pp. 111 ff.

and tribe, for all that, within the family. Indeed, Mackenzie of Rosehaugh goes so far as to say that while a son may take precedence of his father, " it may be doubted, whether though this hold in Employment, it ought to hold in Titles, since in these the Son represents not the Common-wealth ; And therefore in these cases the Laws of Nature ought to prevail above the Laws of Honour, especially, if there be none present but Father and Son ; But if there be a third person present who will take the place from the Father, but not from the Son, then the Son must preceed the Father ; because, though he yeeld to his Father, yet he should not yeeld to a third Party ".[1] As the father is the chief, it is obvious from this, that a Peer cadet within the clan loses his peerage precedency. This is confirmed by his statement that " In Families likewise, the Chief of the Family takes place of any Gentleman of the Family ".[2]

It is incredible, when we consider the mass of evidence which exists, only a part of which we have been able to cite, that some modern English heraldic writers still persist in saying that gentility is not decided by the Laws of Arms.[3] While words can be allowed any precise meaning and logic employed in their use this is palpably false. On the other hand if it be decided to shift the meaning of gentleman from its understood value in nobiliary law and to give it the connotation which it may take on in this generation, and again in that, in popular usage, then all precision and logic can be dispensed with.

To infer (because there is a popular estimation of a gentleman as a man of liberal education, good manners, and some wealth) that gentility cannot be assessed by the assize of arms, is to avoid the whole issue. We are not talking about what is popularly called a gentleman in the recent past or in our own times in England, but what is a gentleman as understood in nobiliary law not only in England, but in other countries as well, and that class of gentility which is ancient nobility, and which is the sole criterion for admission into all society where proofs of nobility are required. Such gentility is assessed by assize of

---

[1] *Observations upon the Laws & Customs of Nations as to Precedency.* Edinburgh, 1680, p. 72.

[2] *Ut supra*, p. 56.

[3] Or failing which by recourse to proof before a Court of Chivalry—where, at some considerable expense, and a great deal of trouble, it is just conceivable that it might be possible to establish the right to gentility by some other evidence in default of that of arms.

L

arms,[1] and in no other way, except in the rare cases of the nobility of
lands which never adopted heraldic devices as the *tesserae nobilitatis*,
such as in the case of Armenia or Greece.

If the term is to be interpreted in the light of the ever changing
current usages of the populace as a whole,[2] and not by the interpretations of the Laws of Arms, then we venture to suggest that the sense
in which such writers still use it (for a well-mannered person living in a
certain style) is already out of date in England—for it is now the term
for all males of 18 years or more of age, of whatever social class,
cultural background, or colour of skin, which has come to replace the
entirely, for the masses, anti-social word *man*, which is not a respectable one to apply to stevedore, although it may still be applied to any
armigerous gentleman.

When the term gentleman is used in a work of armory it is not
concerned with a man's cultural state as such (although this may be
incidental to his being in that nobiliary state which is gentle), nor with
his natural disposition, which has led some to talk of a nature's gentleman, nor with the modern use of the term for the whole of the male
half of the English proletariat, but solely with its use in nobiliary law,
that is the Laws of Arms, and its rank in nobility, as understood throughout most of Christendom from the Middle Ages to the present.   In
resisting any interpretation of nobiliary terms in any other manner

---

[1] Or, as we have just observed above, more rarely by an actual *ad hoc* decision, in each
case as it arises, before a Court of Chivalry.

[2] There are, it should be observed, apart from any other considerations, great disadvantages
in the vehicle of language when words are made of no use, because they are made to lose their
precise meaning and take on ever-changing interpretations by their common abuse, such as
we get so frequently in the English tongue.   One of the obvious disadvantages is that unless
carefully qualified the terms we are discussing have no meaning outside of a book on heraldry,
genealogy or law.   As a consequence the masses cannot designate an actual gentleman
(that is a noble) as understood in nobiliary law.   For the very word they should use has taken
on new, and quite different meanings.

An anecdote of Sir James Lawrence, K.M., well illustrates the results of this curious English
national characteristic of refusing to call things what they are, and underlines some of the
disadvantages which can arise from refusing to be logical in such matters— a " German baron,
in London, having waited for his barber, a journeyman arrived in his stead, and informed
him, that the old *gentleman* had been taken ill, but that he would have the honor of shaving
him ! This anecdote the baron used to relate whenever any Englishman was presented at his
master's court, to insinuate that the English gentry were a set of barbers ".   *Op. cit.*, pp. 122-3.

than as understood in the Laws of Arms, we would observe that we are neither attempting to strip the non-armigerous people of culture nor the masses of the proletariat of their self-assumed grandeurs of nobility. We are here only at pains to understand the ranks of society with which we have been dealing in their historic nobiliary legal signification. In that connotation gentry is an order in nobility which can only readily be assessed by assize of arms, no matter how much some writers may protest to the contrary, as all the evidence we have considered amply proves.

Returning, therefore, to the purposes of this chapter, which we defined at the outset, we have shown that gentry is the state or order of old nobility, and that this latter term is properly speaking the whole *noblesse*, and not to be understood in this work, any more than in ancient writings or international works on heraldry, as confined to the peerage alone.

CHAPTER XIV

THE SOCIAL AND MORAL IMPLICATIONS OF GENTILITY

BEFORE we proceed, in the next chapter, to consider the modern implication of arms outside of the British Isles, it is advisable to pause and consider what has been the social and moral contributions which this armigerous class of nobles has made. It is our intention here, from an examination of all the terms which are used for the armigerous nobility, to indicate that the outcome of such a type of society has been beneficial to the community as a whole, and is, indeed, more so than that stratification of ranks which would appear in a purely capitalist or communist society.

As we have already mentioned earlier the term gentry is derived from *gentrice* from the Old French *genterise* for *gentelise*, which is equivalent to the Latin *generosus* a word derived from the Latin *gentilis*, meaning to belong to a race or *gens*. Thus our *gentleman* is derived from the French *gentilhomme*, meaning a *man of race*. While such as Selden, in his *Titles of Honor*, 1672, states that gentleman is convertible with *nobilis*, this is only so in a general way, as it becomes necessary, as we have seen, to distinguish from time to time between gentry and nobility. In the same way those who say it is equivalent with *adel*, ought to qualify that statement, since its equivalent is *uradel*, *ancient noble* rather than just noble.

Following upon the Black Death (1349) and other causes creating social changes in England younger sons began to seek their fortunes away from the ancestral estates. Thus we begin to find them subscribing themselves as *generosi*. This was hastened in England by the statue of I Henry VI, cap. V., 1413, which laid down that all persons who were defendants in causes of outlawry had to state their rank.

The first actual record of the style gentleman upon any monument is found on that of John Daundelyn of Margate (1445), and the first time it is employed for a member of Parliament in England is in the case of William Weston, *gentylman*, in the latter half of the fifteenth century.

Now the impact of this noble class, among whom the established families were called gentry, is seen in our literature. We know the ideas which *Commissar, Secretary of the Politburo, Moneylender, Banker, Master, Director, Inspector, Upper-Class, Socialite, Rich, Society, Industrialist, Whip, Tycoon, Capitalist, Supervisor, Boss, Gaffer, Manager, Civil Servant,* or any other similar modern terms, call to our minds. They are each in its turn and place, in some way or another, invidious to down-right bad. Each one in some measure or another conjures up some form, from mild to extreme, of oppression, or selfishness, or ruthlessness. Many of us, because of the structure of our society, may be compelled to some degree or another to belong to some such classifications as these, and yet, on reflection, very few would want to see them engraved on their epitaphs.

When we turn to our literature, however, and take this term gentleman, and its cognate words, *gentle, gentry, generosus, generous* and so on, and trace them in their use, we get a far different impression. The mental pictures they recreated in the minds of our forebears, and even in those of ourselves to this day, are almost the opposite from what the terms we have mentioned for the political and ruling classes of today produce.

Thus we find that the word gentleman, from as early as the time of Chaucer (such as in his *Melboeus,* c. 1386, the *Wife of Bath's Tale,* and the *Romance of the Rose,* c. 1400) began to take on a meaning implying a degree of virtue. As time has passed this use of the word has increased in general currency. To behave like a gentleman, or to be of gentlemanly conduct, has come to be a hallmark of virtue. Indeed, the use of the term has become so common, especially in the mouths of moralists, that there is a danger of forgetting its precise and legal meaning in that class which begat these values which we associate with the word.

We may also add that the word *generosity* denoting liberality, is but the Latinised version of the same word, and is the attribute to be associated with a *generosus* or a gentleman. Generosity is used by the older writers to mean gentility. Thus John Bossewell, gentleman, writing in 1572, in his *Workes of Armorie*, Fol. 9, has such expressions as " Vices whiche are repugnant to Generositie ", where we would use gentility today. Then we may take the word *gentle*. What a beautiful word it is. The name of a nobiliary quality, the gentle or well-born, and yet signifiying to behave with kindness and humanity.

The nobles of early feudal Europe were also the freemen (although comprehended in that classification were also the yeomanry, the principal members of which in England were called franklings : another variant of the same word). This word finds its expression in the Latin version in the words *liberal* and *liberality*, and in the Teutonic version, as *frank*,[1] meaning open and fearless, and without guile. All these words are wholly good and pleasant in their connotations.

If we take the term noble, which is comprehensive of all who have arms, we find that this term which connoted a whole class, and a conquering one at that, has come to mean noble in bearing, in mind, in quality of personality, in the sense of upstanding, and a good person. The same term has given rise to the expression *noblesse oblige*. One cannot imagine the expression Commissar-oblige, or Boss-oblige, or Director-oblige, ever gaining any currency.

In countries such as Italy, as we have shown elsewhere, an upper class arms-bearing society grew up in the city states, and their arms are called *arms of civility*. Here again we have a word which although it is not strictly belonging to the feudal nobility, but to an analogous class in the burghs, yet gives rise to at least a desirable connotation which we associate with *civil* conduct, and *civility*.

Out of the nobility arose knighthood, and again the impressions left are all pleasant and desirable ones. We get *knightly* conduct, *chivalry*, *chivalrous*, and so forth. It is true we get *cavalierly* from the same source, meaning to act in an off-hand manner, but this is a later

[1] It may be observed that the *free* comprehended the yeomanry as well as the noblesse, and the word yeoman has, not surprisingly, in view of the general estimation of *frank* and *liberal*, come to have a good meaning. Hence to give *yeoman service* to any cause is highest praise. In contrast to have been a farmer, as distinct from the freehold-farmer (the yeoman or frankling) has given us such words as *boor*, and *boorish* from the actual word for farmer (cf. boer in Afrikaans), and *villain*, from the word for a farm labourer, or the small-holder who lived in the *ville* or township of the manor.

development out of the known fact that knights acted with independence of mind and action. Even the word *squire*, corruption of esquire, after generations of pantomimes with their wicked squire themes, has survived and still retains the kindly and gallant meaning which became associated with it from the class of esquires. Even at its worst meaning today, it is nothing worse than a gallant person acting as an escort to a lady.

We have seen that while *lord* was a general word for leading nobles, not necessarily peers, hence lords of manors, lairds, and so on, it has become restricted largely to an ever increasingly more and more political caucus, associated with parliament. Here only do we strike a nobiliary style which begins to take on an unfortunate tone. To be lordly, does not mean to be gentlemanly or noble-like, but to be pompous and conceited. (In contrast, however, laird has retained its kindly associations.) Lady, the feminine of lord, and of much wider connotation than that of *lord*, for a peer, as in lady of the manor, the chief's lady, the knight's lady, and so on, has retained a pleasant meaning—*She is a real lady* is used with approbation, as if the word were the same as gentleman. Likewise, even dame, for a squire's or a knight's lady, has a kindly ring, even in its lowest social connotation, of *an old dame*. To give it the ugly twist it has to be qualified as *beldam*, when it ceases to be the word derived from a nobiliary rank. *Gentlewoman*, although not much used now, never carries with it a suggestion that is not desirable. *Aristocrat*, a word compounded out of Greek, is not a natural word to western Europe at all, and largely an importation after Renaissance times into our common speech, and mainly confounded with *lord*. Here again we have a meaning which does not belong to the kindly, helpful and good characteristics which arose out of those words which come down to us from the earlier, and widespread, nobility of the land.

It seems hard in view of the cumulative effect which these words make on the mind to escape the conclusion that the social effects of a widespread nobility in the state, such as existed in feudal times very apparently (but which is still with us in a numerous armigerous class, although much less conscious of itself), was wholly good—and much more so than the forces of power which have been thrown up either in

an entirely allegedly egalitarian communistic society, or an equally
allegedly egalitarian society as is found in countries which have either
never had, or have succeeded in entirely suppressing, the nobiliary
foundations of society.

To be a gentleman meant not only to be of ancient lineage. But
it also meant in the times when the nobility as a whole were conscious
of being nobles, that from those so named a high code of conduct was
demanded. This was consciously inculcated from generation to
generation. Selden is no isolated example when he says that a gentleman should not only pride himself on his lineage but that he should
follow the example of that lineage. If this had not been done more
often than not we would have had an entirely different ring to words
like *gentleman*, *gentle*, *generous*, *liberal*, *frank*, *lady*, *chivalrous* and the rest.
The good meanings we attach to these words spring from the fact
that this noble society gave to them, by its conduct, interpretations
which are wholly praise-worthy.

There are also important social considerations which flow from the
continued existence and vitality of a widespread and numerous
noblesse in any society.

Far from a legalistic understanding of the nature and implication
of arms being snobbish (as has been alleged by some English writers
who have failed to grasp its full significance) it is a great redresser of
balances. For, on the one hand, within the nobility as a whole it
allows a proper assessment of the value to be placed on knighthood
and peerage. While, on the other, it denies to those who rely solely
on wealth, political influence, ostentation, and the " old school tie "
complex, acceptance as gentry. As long as they are denied legal
admission to the noblesse of a realm until they have sued out humbly
before the Court of Chivalry the all important letters patent they have
one reminder that wealth and influence alone do not automatically
admit them to everything worth while in this life. While, if they
have the grace to do this, they admit that they must have a beginning.
In that they are prepared to do it in their own persons they have shown
that becoming modesty and humility which is a pre-requisite of being
truly noble.

It will, of course, be said that this redressing of balance is, after all, only within the noblesse and between those socially of the same stratum of society, and does not comprehend more simple folk.   But so far as it spreads to so wide a class as the noblesse, which comprehends nearly all the leaders of any society, it is surely something worth while.   For here we have in it an operative factor, preventing too small a clique, especially in this day when there is a strong tendency for too great a concentration of power to be in the hands of politicians and capitalists, from riding too highly over the rest of the nation.

CHAPTER XV

A COMPARISON OF THE RIGHTS TO ARMS IN VARIOUS MODERN STATES

THE survey which we have now concluded concerning the nature of arms in some of the principal states of Europe from the earlier times, inclusive of their position in such countries as England, Scotland, Ireland and Sweden to the present time, leaves little doubt as to what value is to be placed upon them. Despite the fact that in certain states, such as in France, there may have been contradictory practices and legislation, and in the Empire where arms were once freely used before the heraldic authorities began to impose on them a nobiliary value, there can be little doubt that in most monarchies or other states where courts of chivalry or their equivalents functioned, arms were in some measure or another of nobiliary status, with, in some cases, an extension of something of this character to higher burgher families of distinct civility.

From this it can be said that in England, Ireland, Sweden, Scotland, and the like, arms are related in law and practice to nobility. In Poland, in so far as we consider the position up to the establishment of the Communist regime, arms were restricted to noble families and clans. In Imperial Russia arms were likewise restricted to nobility, and presumably are so regarded by the emigrant Russians. In Portugal the use of arms is restricted to those which were granted or matriculated by authority, and these belonged to noble families.

In Italy, although the monarchy ceases to govern,[1] through the very complete organisation which the nobility has set up, in collaboration with the king, in fact no arms are recognised by the noblesse, except

---

[1] King Umberto never abdicated, does not regard himself as an ex-King, and is not so regarded by the nobility of Italy.

those which conform to the laws of the former realm of Italy, which forbade arms to non-nobles, except for that class of near-nobles, the higher burgher families of distinct civility—whose arms, since they are of record in the *Consulta Araldica*, can be considered as tantamount to those of a civic patriciate with some limitations. San Marino has exactly the same law, and there arms are noble, or of distinct civility.

In Belgium only the arms of nobles and of communities which have been registered in the *Conseil Héraldique du Royaume* are recognised and capable of protection. But in Belgium other arms are used, and these will be dealt with shortly. In Liechtenstein[1] arms are conferred with the titles which are attached to them. Such arms are clearly noble,[2] and are capable of legal protection also.

However, at this point we come to a radical departure from the practices of the realms we have been discussing. We saw earlier that in France there had always been a tendency to use arms more freely than either the nobility or the Crown would normally have countenanced, and that burgher arms, at times, got quite out of hand, and spread a long way beyond those who in Italy or San Marino would have been considered of " distinct civility ". The French heraldic authorities tried to curb these proliferations of arms, but only with ill-success on the whole. The result of this was that after the collapse of the monarchy no machinery has existed to curb the adoption of new arms by all and sundry. That is actually the position today in France.

In France itself there was always a strong tendency to insist upon a difference between the arms of nobles, anobli, and burghers (where the latter obtained them legitimately either in the capacity of having held noble offices or being of distinct civility) since the latter two were not allowed to bear with them any additaments (helm, mantling, wreath, crest, or motto) in addition to the shield. This principle has been continued to the present time, so that whereas there is no law to prevent a general adoption of new arms (which do not infringe those

[1] Jacques Descheemaeker, *Le Droit des Armoiries*, La Vie Judiciaire, 7-12 March 1960, p. 5.
[2] But there are other uses of armorial shields by burghers in accordance with common Germanic practice in this connection which are not noble. These are related to the practice which now occurs in modern France.

of anyone else) such arms do not carry additaments, or coronets, which are recognised as belonging to the noblesse alone.

Despite the fall of the monarchy arms are still subject to legal surveillance before the Courts of France.

Consequently no existing arms can be usurped by later arms, which means in fact that all arms formerly on record under the monarchy are protected, as are titles, although this means that self-created arms by non-nobles would be protected also, provided that their priority over later arms could be established—which is not very easy.[1]   In general, however, such non-noble arms can be distinguished from noble arms by having no form of helm, crest or coronet over the shield.

This practice has, as might well be expected, in view of the influence of French culture and language in Belgium, affected that country to the extent that citizens often assume arms of a like character to those of similar people in France.   But any assumption of additaments, such as a helm or crest are liable to action being taken by the authorities under article 230 of the Penal Code of Belgium.[2]   Consequently the absence of a description of the additaments or of the display of them or the coronet over the arms indicates at once in such a work as the *Armorial General de Belgique*[3] the arms of burghers as distinct from those of noble families.   In Denmark the position is much the same as in Belgium.   Burghers assume arms without prohibition.   But such arms are distinct from those of nobles.

In Spain the arms of the noblesse and of corporations are protected by law, although following the French example it seems that burghers widely use self-created arms.

In the Netherlands, since 1815, the adoption of shields of arms is not specifically forbidden, although, again, as in Belgium, the position is different where the use of additaments associated with noblesse, such as a coronet, crest and helm, and so forth, are concerned.

[1] Jacques Descheemaeker, *op. cit.*, 29th Feb.-7th March, pp. 1 ff. and 7-12th March 1960 pp. 4 ff., explains at length the current legal position of arms in France and the steps necessary to protect them as far as this is possible.

[2] *Ut supra*, 7-12th March 1960, p. 4.

[3] Published under the direction of F. Koller and S. Melia, Brussels.

In all these states it will be observed that generally speaking the arms which are of record in the official registers, are noble arms,[1] which are protected from usurpation in law, and their use is as noble arms, although that distinction is not made absolutely apparent without the use of further additaments; while shields which are not recognised have no protection in law. From this it would suggest that in a large measure, so far as the sovereignties of those states are concerned, they are ignored and to that extent do not exist. The conclusion must, therefore, be in all these cases, except that of France which we have cited, where the position is abnormal through their not being either a monarchy or regency or heraldic officers, that the basic nature of arms, as accepted and recorded by the state, is a nobiliary one—despite the widespread de facto use of shields of arms of varying degrees of questionability by many citizens in some of them.

When we come to Switzerland we are dealing with a state, or a confederation of states, which are not successors of former noble and monarchistic systems of society. Here there is an heraldic adminstration, in a tribunal to judge the right to the bearing of arms. We have indicated earlier that the widespread use of arms in " peasant " (that is freehold farmer or yeoman) societies probably arose from the fact that the lands held were in fact originally feudal fiefs. However that may have been, this led to a widespread use of arms, and consequently it led ultimately to a situation that anyone can take for his family such arms as he pleases without prejudice to the rights of others. These arms in Switzerland, therefore, although probably arising from an originally petty noble fief basis, are clearly no longer noble, nor could be so received by those adminstrations which grant arms as honours from the Crown, or the State.

Passing to the United States [2] we should observe that while there is a widespread adoption of arms, they are not recognised by the State.

---

[1] With the possible exception of France, where for the reasons we have explained earlier burgher arms did, from time to time, come to be recorded—although, even in these cases, some may have been those of people having noble charges.

[2] In America, the Committee on Heraldry of the *New England Historic Genealogical Society* is publishing rolls of arms, composed of the arms which they have registered, and which consist of arms which the bearers show were borne by their names originally, or which they have assumed, provided that they are not the coats of others. Rolls have been issued by them in 1928,

Since in America there is no law to interdict the self-assumption of arms of any kind, such arms as are created in this way cannot be suppressed within that country.   Therefore such arms are neither legal nor are they illegal there—although they are a currency of no value elsewhere where the Law of Arms is still administered, or where public opinion demands standards which only the Law of Arms would sanction.   We are not saying therefore that Americans cannot if they so wish make up such designs on a shield and conforming to heraldic rules of blazon.   All we are saying is that we think that the attempt to give a legal basis to these actions by invoking the law of prescription is not valid, as the conditions necessary for a prescriptive right to arms to be made out do not exist.   In days when prescription could be argued the bearers could come before some tribunal or high authority and argue a prescriptive right to bear such arms.   There is no court before which an American can go and argue his prescriptive right, because his " arms " are no more able to be taken notice of than are rights in any noble arms, since that State has chosen to declare that it does not recognise nor take any cognizance of nobility.   The only way a self-created shield of arms could be protected in American law would be as a trade mark or some similarly registered mark, but not as either noble arms, conveyed by lawful authority in times past, or as arms (whatever their nobiliary status) which had arisen prescriptively.

In Federal Germany a similar situation exists where anyone takes any arms he likes, as there are no specific laws to prevent such assumptions.   Since 1922 there has been an unofficially produced *Heroldausschus der Deutschen Wappenrolle* in which there are recorded such assumptions of arms.   In all cases a brief is issued saying that the arms are recorded for purpose of establishing proof of their existence in cases of civil processes in law.   But such self-assumed arms cannot lawfully carry noble additaments, such as noble helms and coronets.

1932, 1936, 1940, 1946, 1954 and 1958.   The body issuing these has contended that they hold the views of Oswald Barron, that arms are not held of the Crown, but are personal property, " the right to which depends simply upon user and the right as against others upon prior assumption " (Oswald Barron, *The Ancestor*, VI, July 1903, p. 162).   This statement is, without any shadow of doubt, in error where Scottish arms are concerned, since these depend from the Crown as feudalised heritage.   For the views of this American body see—*A Roll of Arms, New England Historic Genealogical Society*, Boston, 1928-1958.

In states under the British Crown, where the Queen reigns as Queen of those countries, the Queen is the Fountain of Honour, whether in fact she confers honours or not.   In Canada, for instance, no titles or ranks of nobility have been granted to Canadian subjects at the request of the Canadian Government.   There has, however, been no interference with the Crown's powers to confer arms, and these are regularly given to Canadian, South African, Australian, New Zealand, and other British subjects.   While, in addition, French-Canadian as well as Maltese nobility (and therefore their arms) are protected and guaranteed by the British Crown by treaties.   Normally petitioners desiring arms in any of these countries apply to one or the other of the Kings of Arms in the British Isles.   However, these Kings of Arms have no actual jurisdiction in these overseas territories and it is doubtful if they could in any way enforce their jurisdictions if they so desired.   On the other hand while ever the British Kings of Arms continue to grant arms in any of these states, the genuine arms drive out the spurious, which have no opportunity of development as in countries absolutely without recourse to a Fountain of Honour for grants of arms.

In conclusion, it can be held as generally established, that arms granted or allowed by a Sovereign have usually been regarded as signifying noble or distinctly civil status, and where originally this was not so, steps have been taken at later stages in the development of such states by the Crown directly or through its heraldic officers, to ensure that such arms were granted as ensigns of nobility.   In particular, the arms granted by the sovereigns of the various British kingdoms have had that connotation, and still have, and in a Scottish patent it is explicitly stated that the arms are a fief noble.

Even where, through the absence of, or defective powers of the Sovereign, or the state, this has not been the case, as in France, the ensigning of the shield of arms with additaments of helm or crest has been evidence of noble status.

Finally, the use of self-assumed arms, either in the past in certain places, or still in Germany, the United States of America, or in France, or arms granted specifically *without nobility*, as in the Empire or in Switzerland, do not constitute what is meant by arms in the context of the Law of Arms as it has been understood in the past, and is still

operatively administered, in any of the British realms which maintain
their heraldic officers and courts of chivalry. Although it is probably
true to say that any charges borne on a shield anywhere, whether
self-assumed or not, or granted freely as in Switzerland, do tend to
signify some sort of status for their bearers, since they have risen
socially to a condition in which they feel the need for armorial-like
ensigns.   Such shields are, however, more to be equated with
Merchants' Marks, or Rebuses, than Arms as understood in the realms
where heraldic law is still administered, since they are freely taken and
discarded, and confer no legally recognised status.   Consequently
they throw no light upon the nature of arms as we understand that
term. Although, since they are on shields, since they employ the terms
of heraldry, since they observe the laws of blazon, and since they are
normally transmitted within a family, they obviously have to be
considered heraldic. For all that they are not arms as they are understood before the Courts of Chivalry and officers of arms.

Since within such a realm as that of Scotland (to take only one
where the Law of Arms is strictly administered in accordance with the
laws, customs and statutes governing heraldry) a shield of arms is a
noble fief, it is necessary that where such Scottish arms have to be
advanced abroad, in birthbriefs, or in proofs of nobility or for any other
cause, they should always be shown with helm and mantling at least,
in order to make it quite clear that they are not to be confused with
non-noble burgher heraldic compositions, such as are found in France,
Belgium and Germany.

Conversely, no Scottish, English, Irish, Swedish, or Italian, or
similar heraldic administration ought to, or can, accept for matriculation in its registers arms from elsewhere without a strict enquiry as to
their status. It is not merely necessary to ascertain whether they are
legally-borne in their country of origin, but what status they confer.
Perfectly legal Swiss arms, or any modern French, even if supported
by pronouncements of the French courts, are not necessarily noble
in character, unless supporting evidence to that effect is produced.
Consequently such arms lacking that specific nobiliary evidence cannot
be matriculated in the registers of realms where the nature of arms is
of noble origin and continues to confer noble status.

A word should be said about the assumption of arms by bishops of either the Episcopal or Roman Catholic Church in such countries as America, India, or other countries where there is no machinery for the control of arms. A bishop, and other grades of clerics also, has the right to arms by reason of his position. He has also the need of arms in respect of his duties. He belongs, in addition, to an order of society where there is a public opinion, as in mediaeval times, capable of taking its own steps to adjust abuses in claims or styles of any ecclesiastic in the Church Courts. Here and here *alone* would it seem that there can be established a *prima facie* case for the prescriptive right to arms which occurs in these instances. Such arms are essentially noble since their bearers are occupying charges which have always been recognised as noble. Nevertheless for their own protection all ecclesiastics who by their rank have need of the use of arms ought, *where the way is open to them*, to seek to obtain their arms from a Sovereign source, rather than to resort to a prescriptive right for them, which is not above being challenged, and under which there can be no protection (outside of their own ecclesiastical courts). It should also be pointed out that such prescriptive right, while it has even been exercised in England in connection with the R.C. archdiocesan arms of Westminster[1], is inhibited in Scotland where the Lord Lyon King of Arms is the sole source of new arms.

---

[1] These arms were granted by Pope Leo XIII in 1894—but since the Pope cannot exercise Sovereignty in the territory of another realm they must be looked upon as a self-assumption in the English Realm by the Roman Catholic archdiocese, whatever may be its own internal arrangements to obtain that grant. For the details of this grant, written from the Roman Catholic point of view, see *The Arms of the Archdiocese of Westminster*, by John A. Goodall, *The Coat of Arms*, Vol. IV, No. 30, April 1957, pp. 241 ff.

M

INDEX

COLOUR PLATES

Examples of Noble Arms from Scotland, England, and Ireland from official Rolls and Records.

PLATE I

The first folio of *Scottish Arms from the 14th Century Armorial de Gelré*

die co
mc va
scorlat

gt de
rog

gt de
car
ric

gtl
de
viue

gt a
fra
ere

gtl
a
ouglas

gtl
de
maerche

gt
de mar

kin
caman

gt
de morref

gt
a
teue
lenos

ananderdeel

PLATE II

The second folio of Scottish Arms *from the* 14th Century Armorial
de Gelré

gtf a
karric

gtf
a srra
de ren

gtf
a asʒol

gtt
a suder
lant

ſyr archibaur

gtf a
orcana

lū
ert a
ſeton

gtf
a ros

ſĩr
bauter a leſlij

ſĩr
roon
ſeneſcal

ſĩr
iā de
lỹndeʒaẏ

ſyr
aleʒ
ſander
ſtulbart

ſĩr
dauid
de lỹndeʒaẏ

lourt
a
leuls

ſyr
roon
n,
abb'natūn

PLATE III

The third folio of *Scottish Arms from the 14th Century Armorial de Gelré*

san
delandis

sir
rub
berr of
erski

sir
lo
urr a
morref

sir
thomas
erskin

sourr
a
reets

sir
allex
ad ranfa

sir
loon of
eet moiton

sir
rob
bert
colleuile

sir
wal
tert
helhborton

sir
her
ri
aprefton

sir
p
comyn

sinclaer

sir patri

PLATE IV

English Grant of Arms to the Drapers' Company of London, 1439

PLATE V

Birthbrief from the Lord Lyon King of Arms, Public
Register of Genealogies, iv. 9, 27th March 1930

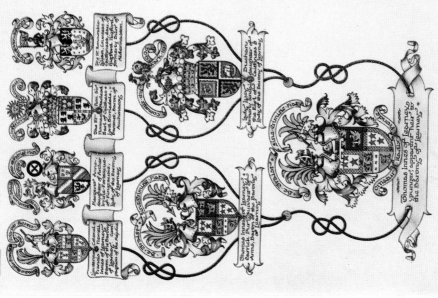

O ALL AND SUNDRY

We Francis James Grant, Esquire, Lord Lyon King of Arms, Do hereby certify that We are satisfied, on an examination of the proofs produced that Thomas Innes of Learney, younger, was born upon the 22nd day of January 1930, and is the son and apparent heir of Thomas Innes of Learney, Carrick Pursuivant of Arms, Baron of the Baronies of Learney and Kinnairdy, Advocate, Member of the Royal Company of Archers, and his wife Lucy Buchan, or Innes of Learney, his wife, who were married upon the 17th December 1928. That Arms were matriculated in the Public Register of All Arms & Bearings in Scotland upon the 3rd day of April 1916 in name of the said Thomas Innes of Learney, elder as heir male and representative of the House and Family of Innes of Learney...

[The remainder of the document consists of densely written heraldic and genealogical text which is not legibly reproducible.]

...Given at Edinburgh, this day...

One thousand nine hundred and thirty.

Thomas J. Grant
Lyon

ARMORIES of Thomas Innes of Learney, younger

PLATE VI

Extract of matriculation : CHARLES IAN FRASER of REELIG

·EXTRACT·OF·MATRICULATION·

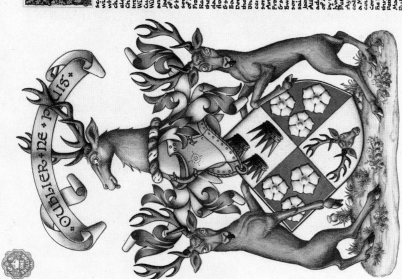

OUBLIER ✦ NE ✦ PUIS

PLATE VII

Extract of matriculation : CHARLES HARRY PIRIE-GORDON of BUTHLAW, O.B.E., O.S.C., G.C.ST.J., showing his standard along with his supporters as a Knight Grand Cross of the Venerable Order of St. John in the British Empire.

of the Arms of BIRSE GORDON of BUCKLAW.

PLATE VIII

Certificate of Arms issued by the Chief Herald of Ireland

Do gach n-aon chun a ttuigfidh

an scríbhinn seo, Bairimbe, Éamonn MacGiollabachla, M.A., —
MRDA, DLitt, Príomh-Aralt na Ríoccann, beannacht, agus déirium a
sheanbhuí a sheasbhú leis seo go mbainnean an tearnad so teanab,
eadhon go ceathrúnach I agus 4: ar nuine, rachtán cuirt-eagach ibte
trí cairt-fhiadhtha ar stánach árdha, file gorm, ar ghrach ceann
siobic (do Robinson): 2 agus 3, ar ghorm, rachtán ibte trí teamtra,
le sazaible, agus obás mhion-ghearathláig árdha (do Lynch)
agus mar Cháirt:- do Mac-chorún árdha crecan nuine go bhfuil
cairt-fhiadh mar olá san teamas ha sheazamh air CroRobinson)
agus Lynch sivluch mealkta airgói, conlóir dearg air, le slabhra
fraith-fhille thar an sron árdha (do Lynch), agus mar Rose Lyn
Rose Fidus, agus a iomlán ban beartha níos Réira ar a
inteall so, go mbainnann só de chearl leis an Aidire Criobóir
Anntaoi Lynch Robinson, Baroinéid.

Dá fhianaibe sin scríobhas m'ainm agus mo Shaibeal leis
seo agus gheamaios Sála m'Oifige she an cúigiú lá so is fichið
so mhí Súil Míle naoi geéas beacht is bachad.

Seul Q fo.42:

Éamonn MacGiollabachla
Príomh-Aralt